Contents

List of Tables   vii
Preface   ix

PART 1

1 **Introduction**   1
  An Area College defined   2
  Jones College   3
  The analytical perspective of the study   4
  The general environment of technical colleges   8
  The technical college as an 'open' institution   10
  The staff as a social group   12
  The problem of organizational identity   13
  Research techniques   17

2 **Official Policy and Technical College Goals**   19
  Levels of work in colleges   20
  Breadth of work in colleges   23
  Conclusion   26

PART 2

3 **Jones College, Its Setting and Development**   29
  A note on further education statistics   31
  Growth and change   31
  The changes analysed   36
  (a) The demand *available*   37
  (b) The demand *wanted*   39
  Conclusion   45

4 **The Staff of Jones College —Some Characteristics**   47
  Background experience and teacher training   47
  Reasons for entering further education   48
  The technical college teacher's role   50
  Teaching   52
  Research and publication   54
  Conclusion   56

5 **The Staff Climate of Activity**   59
  Promotion   60
  The 'rat race'   64
  The departments and social relationships   65
  Educational qualifications and industrial experience   71
  Conclusion   75

6 **The Staff and the College Goals**   81
   Degree work   81
   Junior work   88
   The character of the work   94
   General education, vocational training and recreation   94
   Conclusion   98

PART 3

7 **Summary and Conclusion**   101

References in the Text
   Books and Articles   109
   Official Documents   111

A Selection from Other Works Consulted   113
Appendices
   I.   Student hours: 1951/2–1966/7   119
   II. Comparative growth rates: Jones College and England
        and Wales   120
   III. Extracts from an interview with a senior college administrator   122
   IV. The main teaching staff sample   124
   V.   The interviewing schedule   125

Conflict and Change in a Technical College

301·55

Beryl F. A. Tipton

University of London Institute of Education

6677

 HUTCHINSON EDUCATIONAL

HUTCHINSON EDUCATIONAL LTD
3 Fitzroy Square, London W1

London Melbourne Sydney Auckland
Wellington Johannesburg Cape Town
and agencies throughout the world

First published 1973

*This book has been set in Univers type, printed in Great Britain
on smooth wove paper by Anchor Press, and bound by
Wm. Brendon, both of Tiptree, Essex*

ISBN 0 09 115981 4

List of tables

Table	1	Student Enrolments	32
Table	2	Distribution of Student Hours between Types of Courses	33
Table	3	Levels of Work	33
Table	4	Distribution of Work between Departments by Quantity	35
Table	5	Distribution of Work between Departments by Quality	36
Table	6	Full time Work Experience	47
Table	7	Teacher Training	47
Table	8	Reasons for entering Further Education	48
Table	9	College Time spent on Administration	50
Table	10	Staff Grades	59
Table	11	Staff Qualifications	59
Table	12	Avenues of Promotion	61
Table	13	Motives for running Short Courses	63
Table	14	Contact between Members of different Departments over College Business	66
Table	15	Visiting among the Staff	71
Table	16	Attitudes to Degree Courses	81
Table	17	Attitudes to Degree Work by Educational Qualifications of the Staff	82
Table	18	Attitudes to the Transfer of Lower Level Work	88
Table	19	Attitudes by Educational Qualifications of the Staff to the removal of Lower Level Work	89

Acknowledgements

This monograph is based on a thesis submitted to the University of Reading for the degree of Master of Philosophy.
The editors of *Research in Education* are thanked for permission to reproduce material first appearing in an article in that journal.
I am very grateful to the members of the college concerned for participating in the project and only wish that I was able to mention them by name. I should like to record my thanks also to Martin Albrow and Viola Klein for their encouragement, and to my husband, Colin, for extensive script reading as well as his encouragement.

Preface

Recent Developments

Not a great deal has happened with regard to published research on the technical college since work began in 1965 on the study of an area college presented here, so that the remarks on the literature of the field made in the introduction to the thesis upon which this Brunel Monograph is based, and to be found in the present Introduction, still seem to apply. In sociology, however, there has been an interesting development: this is the attention being paid to phenomenology. In this country David Silverman's *The Theory of Organisations* points the way to its relevance for the study of organisations but, of course, this was published after our work was completed and therefore was not able to benefit it.[1]

An Overview

The following comments on our objectives, findings and conclusions are intended for the general reader who only wishes to briefly familiarise himself with the Monograph's contents.
The primary objective of the study was to look at the technical college from an angle largely overlooked, from the inside. Writers on further education have a habit of concentrating upon the forces that play upon colleges, such as industry, government policy and developments in other sectors of education.[2] This, we believe, has had two consequences. Firstly, general ignorance of what technical colleges are like as social organisations and, secondly, the production of inaccurate histories of the development of further education.
One thing that is peculiar about the post-war English technical college, especially the area college, is the multi-purpose educational function it has acquired, and began to acquire from the start with the 1944 Education Act. We became particularly interested in the meaning of this for its staff structure. For in the heterogeneity of their educational and occupational backgrounds, its members of staff are probably unlike those of any other type of educational institution in the country. To put it another way, the college's staff structure is almost a microcosm of the country's social divisions featuring, as it does, all of the following: graduates and non-graduates; industrially experienced and non-experienced; craftsmen, white-collar workers, managers, scientists, social scientists and artists; men and women; and the relatively young through to the relatively old.

[1] D. Silverman, *The Theory of Organisations*, London (1970).
[2] Typical examples are: M. Argles, *South Kensington to Robbins*, London (1964); A. J. Peters, *British Further Education*, Oxford and London (1967); L. M. Cantor and I. F. Roberts, *Further Education in England and Wales*, London (1969).

However, it might be thought that such differences among the staff had no real meaning for the life of the college: that they were overlaid by strong common bonds, these having been there from the outset or acquired during the course of working in further education. On the basis of our findings at Jones College we cannot hold this view. At Jones, and we have no reason to believe that the college was unusual, it seemed almost as if everything in the situation conspired to prevent the staff, as a whole, having a strong sense of unity. To begin with there was the usual low incidence of teacher training for the further education sector. This meant that the college itself became the main agent of socialisation into the world of technical teaching for its staff. However, the college gave the staff a fragmented experience: they were divided by the layout of buildings, by their organisation into separate departments, by their timetables and by the variation in the intrinsic qualities of their work – craftsmen taught students who were to become craftsmen, graduates taught students who hoped to go to university, and so on. The formal structure of the college, therefore, invited staff to feel different from one another rather than alike. And we argue that the formal structure was a significant influence on staff relationships overall.

The college would have had to exert a very powerful influence, we believe, to have succeeded in unifying its staff. For one of the most surprising findings of the research was the way in which these teachers explained why they entered further education. Not one person in the sample of teachers selected for intensive interviews, when asked about this, gave an answer of the 'teaching as a vocation' kind one might expect. In other words, these were men and women who made no bones of the fact that they had to earn their living. This being so, they were unlikely to be the kind of people who would stand by and allow policies detrimental to their interests pass without a word. And yet there was no one policy for the college that could equally satisfy all their interests.

The nineteen-sixties were a testing time for technical colleges in the middle of the further education structure: it was then that it became clear to many people in such colleges that a choice had to be made. Either the colleges remained multi-purpose institutions but jeopardised their chances of running advanced courses, or they phased out their low level courses so as to stand a reasonable chance of being selected as centres for large proportions of advanced work. Here we see that staff conflict over the goals of a college like Jones was almost inevitable.

Another peculiarity of the technical college is the character of the teaching. The study, we feel, supports our hunch that the act of teaching in a technical college of the Jones type is often less intrinsically satisfying than it is in many other educational institutions. One reason for this is the repetitious and fragmented quality of the work – this being a consequence of, respectively, short courses and a large student turnover, and the part-time and sandwich system of attendance. Another is that many members of staff are confronted with too many students for close relationships to develop between them as a regular phenomenon.

It was part of our stock of held beliefs about teachers that they regarded administration as a deflection from their proper path of duty, namely teaching. It came as a surprise to us, therefore, to find that there was no overwhelming hostility to administration at Jones. And we can only conclude that one reason for this may be that teaching was insufficiently satisfying for these teachers to resent the intrusion of administration into their job. (In the study we go on to discuss the implications of the character of the work itself and the technical college teacher's role for the staff structure and college climate.)

In mentioning administration we touch upon our other opening point, namely that neglect of the insides of colleges has led to inaccurate histories of the development of further education. Administration, the staff felt, was the main avenue to promotion in the college. This may sound strange. We usually regard administration as that that is handed out to the newly promoted man. But they felt that it was not so much qualifications or publications, or least of all good teaching, that took one up the college ladder as the opportunity to demonstrate that one could handle administrative work. In other words, one made one's job and was then promoted into it. An important point is that by administration staff meant, among other things, the launching and management of college courses – the growth nub of the college.

Thus we maintain that the development of colleges has not been merely the result of their passive responses to government policy and market demand. College staffs have engaged actively in matters by selecting policies and markets. Close examination of the development of Jones College indicated that it chose to let demand for some courses go unheeded and engaged in determined efforts to induce the market's interest in others, and this sometimes more in spite of government policy than in response to it. The rise and fall of courses was too important to the staff for it to be conceivable that they would not put their own interpretation upon government policy and demand. Seen in this way, therefore, further education's development becomes the product of a process of *interaction* between government policy, the market and colleges.[3]

In fact, having looked closely at post-war government policy, especially for how it has affected the area college, we have come to the conclusion

[3] This point is developed slightly further in B. F. A. Tipton, 'Some organisational characteristics of a technical college', *Research in Education*, 7, page 11 (1972).

that its vague and incoherent character contributed to the process of self-determination on the part of the individual college. A college could not have operated without making its own decisions about the meaning of government recommendations and how to implement them, and without choosing between the vast numbers of recommendations it received over the period.

College Management

The strength of the post-war system of near laissez-faire in further education is that energetic colleges, like Jones, struck out and developed. This obviously benefited their staffs but in all probability students would not otherwise have had the same number and variety of courses. The weakness of it lies in unnecessary duplication of courses at public expense and some unnoticed devolution of power onto college staffs to determine on what kinds of courses money should be spent. (We are not, therefore, with this latter point, necessarily questioning the ability of staff to make good decisions but the fact that their power in the situation went unrecognised by the world at large.) A final conclusion on the rights and wrongs of the case must hinge upon one's own philosophy. As to the future of college management, the study does raise one point that we consider is worth a special mention. It concerns work satisfaction. As may be recalled from what was said in the previous overview, we felt, on the teaching side of their job, this was somewhat wanting for the staff of Jones College.

The study of work satisfaction in the industrial field is now such a regular pursuit of social scientists and management consultants that it is perhaps rather surprising that despite all the exhortation to the educational sector to raise its productivity (whether this be seen in terms of educating children better or more cheaply), little attention has been given to teachers' work satisfaction. The various official reports always say plenty about the needs of the pupil, student or industrial client, but rarely think through in detail at the same time the consequences of their recommenda-tions for the teacher. With respect to the further education sector there has been in recent years, for example, the Henniker-Heaton Report on day-release, the Industrial Training Act, and the White Paper on Polytechnics, all carrying fundamental implications for the character of the technical college teacher's job and yet, at most, considering these only superficially. This uni-dimensional approach to educational policy making, that is, this habit of concentrating upon the needs of the client to the exclusion of those of the teacher, is short-sighted because it overlooks the fact that education is the product of interaction between teacher and client.

PART 1

1. Introduction

As a glance at the bibliography of any recent textbook on organisations will indicate, for example, *Formal Organizations* by Blau and Scott,[1] making models of and conducting research into organisations is an activity that has grown apace in recent years. This exercise would reveal also that the business firm no longer dominates completely the attention of researchers, that such subjects as prisons and hospitals attract their interest too. However, the educational field, at least in this country, remains only scantily touched by the researcher using an organisational perspective.[2] Probably the English technical college has been neglected in this respect even more than have schools and universities.[3]

One exception is a study of the problems facing a technical college's management and production engineering department made by Sofer and Hutton.[4] However, these authors were interested in the relationship of the department to industry and thus they do not tell us anything about the general structural aspects and the internal dynamics of colleges. More information of this kind is available in the study of Mackinton Technical College by Ethel Venables.[5] Again, however, Lady Venables did not so much set out to analyse the structure of a college as to examine those factors that had a bearing on the educational performance of technical college students. Thus, interaction among members of staff did not receive a great deal of her attention.

Our primary aim has been to add to the stock of knowledge on the English technical college and to this end a particular area college was subjected to detailed analysis to discover the nature of its development and some of the characteristics of its structure. It must be added, however, that there has been no attempt to look at a college as a whole. It was felt that, given the limited resources of the single research worker,

[1] P. Blau and W. R. Scott, *Formal Organizations,* London (1963).

[2] For a similar viewpoint, see E. Hoyle, 'Organisational Analysis in the Field of Education', *Educational Research,* **7,** pages 97–114 (1965).

[3] G. S. Brosan, whilst Principal of Enfield College of Technology, suggested that the reason for this dearth of knowledge was that 'anyone who exposed the power structure of a college was likely to make enemies and have cause to travel'. (G. S. Brosan, 'The Government of Technical Colleges', a paper given to the 1966 National Educational Conference – Further Education Section.) Although this may account for the lack of publications emanating from inside the technical college system itself, it does not explain why there is an absence of researchers operating from bases outside.

[4] C. Sofer and G. Hutton, *New Ways in Management Training,* London (1958).

[5] E. Venables, *The Young Worker at College,* London (1967). This book did not appear until after our research was well under way.

to do this would produce somewhat superficial results and that a better
contribution could be made by choosing, for detailed study, a facet of
college life that had been most neglected. In practice this has meant that
our attention has been directed to the staff of the college and the students
have been left as part of an amorphous 'demand' factor.

Of course there is the bigger issue here of the usefulness of the one-case
study itself.[6] Given the present state of sociological knowledge about
technical colleges, we have no hesitation in using the common argument
that this work provides useful background material for future comparative
studies. However, it is hoped that the study will also be a contribution
to the general stock of knowledge on organisational dynamics.

Definition of an Area College

A Ministry of Education Circular issued in 1956[7] describes the technical
college system as consisting of four types of college – local, area and
regional colleges and colleges of advanced technology. The latter, made
responsible at that time for the system's most advanced work, notably the
sandwich-based Diploma in Technology, have been converted into
university status institutions in recent years. With this exception the
circular's description of the functions of these colleges holds quite well
as an account of the current technical college structure. The idea of
concentrating new full-time advanced work in a selected number of
colleges, to be called Polytechnics, had not had time to have any
fundamental effect on it at the time this research was under way.[8]

The regional colleges are described in the circular as colleges doing
'a substantial amount of advanced work, including in particular full-time
and sandwich courses', but having insufficient amounts to make it
realistic for them to concentrate on such work. Local colleges, on the
other hand, are described as those concentrating on elementary work
and in the main dealing with the part-time student. The area college, the
circular continues, provides 'in addition to the type of course provided
at local colleges, varying amounts of advanced work (i.e. work about the
level of Ordinary National Diploma or Certificate or their equivalent),
mainly of a part-time nature'. Some also, it added, 'offer a few advanced
full-time or sandwich courses'.

[6] *cf.* N. Mouzelis, *Organisation and Bureaucracy,* London (1967), pages 66–70.
[7] Ministry of Education. *The Organisation of Technical Colleges,* Circular 305 (1956).
[8] *cf.* Department of Education and Science, *A Plan for Polytechnics and
other Colleges,* Cmnd. 3006 (1966).

2

Jones College[9]

Jones College, the area college used for this study, fell into the latter category, that is, it was one of those area colleges offering both elementary and advanced courses and on part-time and full-time bases. However, the real diversity of the college's function cannot be appreciated from this. Perusal of the 1967–8 prospectus reveals that it provided all of the following: courses for full-time, sandwich, block-release, part-time and day and evenings only students. Courses lasting for an evening, a day, a week or for various lengths of time up to three years.[10] Courses with predominantly academic, vocational or recreational objectives.[11] Courses requiring as an entrance qualification a degree or a higher national certificate or diploma.[12] Courses open to anyone over school leaving age.[13]

To fulfil this wide range of educational objectives, a teaching staff consisting of people with a variety of specialisms was required. But if the staffing was complicated, the administration was possibly even more so. The arrangement of timetables and classroom accommodation was intricate, the number of examining bodies to take into account was large and the equipment required to meet the needs of such an array of courses was multifarious. In addition, the college dealt not just with its

[9] The real name of the college used for the case-study will not be disclosed for the usual reasons and from now on it will be referred to as Jones College.

[10] The following examples, chosen at random from the prospectus, illustrate this range of bases upon which courses could be attended:
Cutting tool materials – a one-day course;
Queues: their measurement and solution – a one-week full-time course;
London Chamber of Commerce Private Secretary's Diploma – two evenings a week for one year;
Chemical Technician's Advanced Certificate – a one-day and two evenings a week for two years;
Higher National Diploma in Business Studies – either a three-year sandwich course of a two-year full-time course.

[11] *cf.* the following examples taken from the prospectus:
Ordinary and Advanced level General Certificate of Education;
B.Sc. (Econ.), Part 1;
Carpentry and Joinery Craft Certificate Course;
Engineering Planning, Estimating and Costing;
Cookery for the Hostess;
Physical Fitness for Women.

[12] *cf.* for example:
Licentiateship of the Institute of Physics;
Post Graduate Diploma in Management Studies.

[13] *cf.* for example:
Ordinary Level General Certificate of Education;
Drama.

3

students, but also, in some cases, with the firms for whom they worked. Finally, the college had to justify itself, educationally and financially, both to local and central government authorities and this created a need for record-keeping and data collection in order to supply evidence of what had happened and to support any plans for the future. Thus it is no exaggeration to say that Jones College was an organisation of a complex kind.

The Analytical Perspective of the Study

As a broad introduction to our objective we probably cannot do better than to reproduce a comment made at one time by Philip Selznick when justifying his own approach:

> 'Among the practical aims, and theoretical puzzles, of modern social science is the assessment of human institutions. Whether we speak of a trade union, a political party, a school, a business, a government agency, or any other complex enterprise, we wish to know what goals or objectives can be attributed to it, what capabilities it has, what strategies it lives by, and what its probable line of evolution may be.'[14]

As far as Jones College specifically is concerned, there were two sociological problems that caught our attention at the beginning. The first of these has to do with the official goals of, or policy towards, technical colleges. The 1944 Education Act and subsequent official recommendations gave colleges very vague and very diffuse goals on which to act.[15] We were interested in finding out about the actual activities pursued by a college in the face of such loose guidelines and in establishing why it developed in the way it did.

The English technical college tends to be treated as a product of demand.[16] It is true that the 1944 Act did require local authorities to provide such facilities as the community demanded and that there has been no form of legal compulsion on any part of the community to attend technical colleges. However, it seemed to us an unreal interpretation to regard the individual college's part in its development as an entirely passive one, to see it as merely responding in an automatic manner to such requests as emerged spontaneously from among the community.

Having been formally established by legal proclamation rather than by

[14] P. Selznick, *The Organizational Weapon. A Study of Bolshevik Strategy and Tactics, Illinois* (1960) (first published 1952), page v.
[15] *cf.* Chapter 2.
[16] *cf.* S. Cotgrove, *Technical Education and Social Change,* London (1958).

4

direct demand, there was no surety that a college would be immediately faced by a body of potential users. There seems little doubt that it would have to make known its presence in the community and, to some degree at least, induce a demand for its courses. Should the demand eventually outstretch the capacity of a college, and it must be remembered that finance was a problem for local authorities in the postwar era, the college would have to select the needs to be met. In both of these cases, individuals at the college level would be put into a position of having to decide what the college was in fact to do.

The second problem concerns the staff structure of Jones College, one, however, that bears directly upon the first. As we have said, the official recommendations made to colleges were sweeping in their educational objectives. On inspection it became quickly clear that Jones College had acquired a multiplicity of educational functions. One of the unforseen consequences of such a development was that the college had acquired a body of staff characterised by a considerable heterogeneity of educational qualifications and occupational experience. We were interested in the meaning of this for the college. Selznick has said elsewhere that

> 'Every formal organization . . . attempts to mobilize human and technical resources as means for the achievement of its ends. However, the individuals within the system tend to resist being treated as means. They interact as wholes, bringing to bear their own special problems and purposes.'[17]

Both because of this general human characteristic and for the particular reason that staff involvement in decision-making seemed inevitable in technical colleges as the result of the vague official guidelines given to them, the interests and attitudes of the Jones College staff were important. What of course we wanted to know, therefore, was whether the diversity of their backgrounds was reflected in a diversity of interests and attitudes in the college context.

We have set out some of the dimensions of our study in this way not because we are confident that their complete significance has been successfully established but so as to provide some indication of the nature of our enquiry. This will receive amplification later in the Introduction when a few of the factors that relate to the context and character of the technical college in this country are discussed. For the moment, however, more general methodological questions will be dealt with.

One of the main analytical tools used for this study has been the concept of the organisational goal. In view of the connotations attached to this

[17] P. Selznick, *TVA and the Grass Roots. A Study in the Sociology of Formal Organizations,* Berkeley and Los Angeles (1949), page 251.

term some explanation of its present usage is called for.[18] To gain a perspective for this a little time will be spent on describing Etzioni's view on how to study organisations.

Etzioni has strongly criticised researchers in the field of organisational analysis for adopting what he calls a 'goal model' approach.[19] By this he says he means the practice of ascertaining what the goals of an organisation are and then deciding how effective the organisation is in achieving them. He maintains that the results of such an approach are stereotyped: the researcher usually concludes that the organisation does not realise its goal effectively and/or the organisation has different goals from those it claims to have.

It should be noted that Etzioni is not attacking the idea of attempting to measure organisations for the effectiveness with which they achieve their goals. Rather, he is complaining about the restricted model that is being used for the purpose. Thus the 'system model', the approach he recommends the researcher to adopt, is designed to overcome these restrictions. With it, the starting point of an investigation is not the goal but

> 'a working model of a social unit which is capable of achieving a goal'[20]

and the researcher's prime task is that of deciding how close the allocation of resources in the organisation approaches an optimum distribution.[21]

There are two things to note about the position Etzioni finally takes up here. Firstly, the researcher's task is still that of measuring the effectiveness of the organisation in reaching its goals and, secondly, the

[18] cf. M. Albrow, 'The Study of Organizations – Objectivity or Bias?' in J. Gould (ed.), Penguin Social Sciences Survey, 1968, Harmondsworth (1968), pages 146–167, for a detailed analysis of the biases that have crept into the sociology of organisations from dependence upon this concept.

[19] A Etzioni, 'Two Approaches to Organizational Analysis: a Critique and a Suggestion', Administrative Science Quarterly, **5**, 2 (1960), pages 257–278.

[20] A. Etzioni, 'Two Approaches to Organizational Analysis', op. cit. page 261.

[21] Etzioni believes the system model is more satisfactory than the goal model for three reasons. Firstly, as the researcher first surveys the organisation, there is less dependence upon his initial assumptions about the goals of the organisation. Secondly, it takes into account the fact that organisations have to devote some of their energies to activities not related directly to their goals, such as maintenance and obtaining means. And thirdly, by concentrating upon how the resources are distributed, it enables the researcher to avoid the trap of failing to recognise that organisations often have goals that are too utopian when set beside the actual resources available for achieving them.

structure of the organisation is examined not as an end in itself but as a means of answering the goal question.[22] In this study of Jones College, however, no attempt has been made to identify the goal, or goals of the college as such nor, as a consequence, is it measured for goal achievement. Instead the organisational goal has been essentially problematic, an object of analysis in itself, as well as – in turn – a tool of analysis. Thus structure and goals have been used to throw light upon one another.

The organisational goal, therefore, has been treated as a complex concept. This complexity is neatly summarised, however, by Charles Perrow, who has invented the categories 'official goals' and 'operative goals' to cover practically all the facets of organisational life that could come under the umbrella of the term 'goals'.[23] Perrow says that

> 'Official goals are the general purposes of the organisation as put forth in the charter, annual report, public statements by key executives and other authoritative pronouncements.'[24]

But, he continues

> 'Official goals are purposely vague and general and do not indicate two major factors which influence organisational behavior: the host of decisions that must be made among alternative ways of achieving official goals and the priority of multiple goals, and the many unofficial goals pursued by groups within the organisation.'[25]

All this he covers by the term 'operative goals', that is, operative goals indicate what is actually going on notwithstanding the official statements about an organisation's purpose. Operative goals may, of course – as Perrow himself says – either support, subvert, or be irrelevant to official goals.

Turning briefly to the question of organisational structure, once this broad interpretation of organisational goals is adopted, particularly once one comes to regard the official purposes of an organisation as potentially indefinite or imprecisely formulated, then the origins of the formal structures of organisations becomes a more open debate. As Martin Albrow has said, the orthodox goal-orientated definition of an

[22] This is not to imply that elsewhere Etzioni may not adopt different perspectives.
[23] C. Perrow, 'The Analysis of Goals in Complex Organisations', *American Sociological Review,* **25,** 6 (1961), pages 854–866.
[24] *Ibid.* page 855.
[25] *Ibid.*

organisation, namely that it is

> 'a social unit explicitly established for the achievement of specific goals'[26]

makes the formal structure a consequence of the specific, and initiating, goals of the organisation. But if an organisation starts its life with only a vague official purpose, then it is difficult to see, on a common-sense level, how a precise set of arrangements can be laid down from above at the start for carrying out its tasks. In other words, a growth process in the formation of formal structures needs to be recognised. Once this perspective is adopted, the relationship between the play of social forces within organisations and the development of their formal structures comes fully into focus for the researcher.

The General Environment of Technical Colleges

It is difficult to appreciate the room for manœuvre available to the staff of a technical college unless the educational and general social and economic context of the English technical college since the second world war is known. The following points are intended to give some idea of the environmental position. Firstly, the relative economic prosperity of the postwar years has encouraged the practice of staying on in the educational system beyond the compulsory school-leaving age.[27] Technical colleges, in addition to exerting an attraction for the school leaver in their own right, in this respect, have also taken the overflow of the school and university systems. They have been grammar school substitutes for secondary modern pupils and last resorts for unsuccessful university applicants.[28]
Contributing to this pool of would-be university students in the early part of the period was the scheme of student grants made available to discharged ex-servicemen.[29] A third factor increasing the pressure on places in the educational system generally has been overseas students. The Robbins Report, for example, says that in 1961–2, 15 per cent of the students in full-time further education (that is, excluding universities and teacher training colleges) were overseas students.[30]
These three points concern the demand for education as a general force

[26] Albrow, *op. cit.* page 153.
[27] *cf.* Report of the Central Advisory Council for Education (Crowther Report), **1,** paras. 68–71, pages 45–47 (1959).
[28] *cf.* E. Robinson, *The New Polytechnics,* London, pages 18–21 (1968).
[29] *Ibid.* pages 18–19.
[30] Report of the Committee on Higher Education (Robbins Report), Cmnd. 2154, para. 47, page 15 (1963).

in society. However, the technical colleges are unique in the English educational system for their strong relationship with industry and commerce. In 1954, 3·2 per cent only of the relevant age group entered university in Britain and this figure had risen to no more than 4·0 per cent in 1962.[31] A large number of these graduates would enter occupations not directly connected with industry and commerce, such as education, medicine and the civil service.[32] Thus the technical colleges have had almost complete responsibility for post-school formal education and training for industry, commerce and allied occupations.[33] The fourth point, the process of technical and organisational change in the post-war economy, a process which faced employers with new needs in skills — scientific, technical, managerial and professional — and employees with the decline in importance of old skills and the rise of new areas of job opportunities, needs to be looked at, therefore, in the light of this educational situation.[34]

Fifthly, there has been the continuation of the process of professionalisation; the fragmentation of old and the growth of completely new professional bodies, particularly in the field of management and management services in this period, entrance to both old and new having become increasingly dependent upon the possession of educational qualifications.[35] Coupled with this movement there has been the general increase in the reliance placed by employers upon educational qualifications as occupational selection devices.[36]

Finally, the market for the technical college's recreational facilities deserves consideration. In the post-war period there are two factors that have affected the colleges in this respect particularly. One is the general rise in living standards. This point can be illustrated in very concrete terms. Phenomena such as the growth in car ownership, home ownership and holidaying abroad have been accompanied by the growth of courses in

[31] Robbins Report, op. cit. pages 18–19.

[32] Of first degree graduates graduating in 1962, only 24 per cent entered industry and commerce at home. This percentage rose to 25 per cent in 1967. (cf. University Grants Committee, University Development 1962–67, Cmnd. 3820 Table 10, page 23 (1968).

[33] Other institutions that will have provided some additional formal educational facilities included the armed forces, privately run secretarial colleges and correspondence course colleges and publicly owned specialised institutions such as art colleges.

[34] cf. P. M. Musgrave, Technical Change, the Labour Force and Education, Oxford, 1967, Chapter 11; P. Venables, 'The demand for technical education in the United Kingdom' in The World Year Book of Education 1965, The Education Explosion, London, pages 236–239 (1965).

[35] cf. G. Millerson, The Qualifying Associations, London (1964) Appendices I and II, pages 221–258; S. Cotgrove, 'Education and Occupations', The British Journal of Sociology, 13, 1, pages 33–35 (1963).

[36] cf. The Crowther Report, op. cit. para 73, page 48.

colleges on such subjects as car maintenance, painting and decorating for the amateur, foreign languages and French cooking. The other is the changes that have taken place in the position of some women in our society. Modern housing and housekeeping techniques, and the increased participation of husbands in family duties, for instance, have no doubt given more women opportunities to attend technical college courses.[37]

Thus the period with which we are concerned is one in which the potential demand for technical college courses was expanding, and expanding both in quality and scope. It was, in other words, a period of potentially constant growth and change for colleges. And because it was possible for a college not only to grow in size but to change its scope of activity the situation was ripe for conflict over what path in fact should be followed.

The Technical College as an 'Open' Institution

A. Etzioni's conceptual work on the Israeli boarding school is a useful starting point for understanding the function of the technical college.[38] A boarding school is a 'closed' institution, says Etzioni, that is, it is an institution that 'endeavours to provide for most of the physical and psychological needs of its pupils'.[39] And as it has this comprehensive responsibility, he continues, staff have a task that, in its all-embracing quality, resembles the relationship between parents and children.

If one thinks of educational institutions as constituting a continuum, with the 'closed' type at the one end having the maximum responsibility for its young people and an 'open' type at the other having the least amount, then the area college would need to be placed towards the 'open' end of this continuum.

Technical college clients are not young children, indeed they can be older than members of staff and they do not live on the college premises. Thus the conditions for the substitute parent role of the boarding school are missing. However, the structure of the teacher-student relationship for the college is more limited than it is for non-boarding

[37] cf. V. Klein, *Britain's Married Women Workers,* London (1965), page 16, and, by the same author, 'Working Wives', *Institute of Personnel Management, Occasional Papers,* 15, page 13.

[38] A. Etzioni, 'The Organizational Structure of "Closed" Educational Institutions in Israel', *Harvard Educational Review,* **27,** 2 (1957), pages 107–125.

[39] *Ibid.* page 107. Etzioni's term 'closed' is equivalent to that of 'total' used by other writers, cf. E. Goffman, 'On the Characteristics of Total Institutions', in his *Asylums,* New York (1961), pages 1–124. Thus it must be distinguished from B. Bernstein's usage in 'Open schools, open society?', *New Society,* pages 351–353 (1967).

schools. Where short courses are concerned,[40] the teacher may be responsible for a student for no more than one or two hours in all. The majority of the area college's students attend for just one day or one evening a week and for the teacher this means having a particular student for one or two hours a week for, probably, a year.[41] Sandwich students, who with full-time students make up the remaining portion of the intake, will be seen for only two of the year's three terms.[42]

Thus the college makes only a partial contribution to the satisfaction of a student's physical and psychological needs, families, firms, sports clubs, and so on, being additional contributors; whilst the college lecturer is only one person among many in a position to provide advice or give emotional support to the student.

From the viewpoint of the teacher, one of the consequences of these short or fractured staff-student relationships is that there is small opportunity for him to get to know his students. Another is that in order to achieve a complete timetable (a grade B assistant lecturer can have a load of up to 24 class contact hours), a teacher has to deal with a large number of classes. The school teacher will see the same classes several times a week for a year or maybe more; the university teacher will have only a small number of classes, in all, each week and these he will take for at least a year. The area college teacher, because many classes are seen once a week only, will see fresh classes each day of the week and a class seen one week may be replaced by a different one the next (as courses can be of less than a year's duration). Thus he will deal with a large and frequently changing body of students during the course of an academic year and is unlikely to see any of these students for more than a year. Irrespective of the problem of time, therefore, the likelihood that the area college teacher will enter into deep relationships with his students is limited because of the inordinate amount of physical

[40] Short course definitions: according to the Department of Education and Science a full-time short course is a course lasting for up to and including 18 weeks; a day part-time or evening short course, according to the Jones College local authority, is a course lasting for up to and including 12 hours of tuition.

[41] Even when a subject appeared in a course for more than a year it was not automatic practice to try and achieve the continuation of particular staff-class combinations, a point which some members of staff raised themselves in the course of interviews.

[42] A course organised on a sandwich basis is one in which the student attends the college for two terms and works in a firm for the rest of the year. The terms chosen for college attendance vary according to the arrangements made between the college and the firm. There is another type of sandwich course, termed the 'thick' sandwich, which consists of longer periods of college attendance but this was not in operation at Jones College.

and psychological energy required where such large numbers of students are involved.

Bryan Wilson has said that,

> 'Because of the diffuse, affective character of the teaching role there is, in contemporary society, a most significant role-conflict arising from the divergence of role-commitment and career-orientation. The teacher is – like everyone in contemporary society – exposed to the pressure to "get on". Achievement and social mobility are the accepted cultural goals of our society . . . Yet the teaching role demands the cultivation of sustained relationships with particular children, and this necessarily means a continued commitment to a particular situation. But the teacher . . . ought to want to "move on to a better job", according to our widely accepted social values.'[43]

We have suggested that the area college teacher's role is more specialised than teaching roles elsewhere in the educational system and that the structure of the teaching situation in the area college does not encourage, or even permit on some occasions, the development of sustained relationships between teacher and student. Thus there is less basis for the conflict between career orientation and commitment to students that, according to Wilson, marks out the teacher. This suggests that a high degree of career orientation is likely to characterise the climate of the area college.

Whether in fact the climate of a particular college will be of this character will depend upon many other factors, of course, but given a situation conducive in other ways to career advancement it is not to be expected that members of the technical college would be unduly inhibited by such normative aspects of the teaching role.

The Staff as a Social Group

In contrast with other British educational institutions, the staff of the area college have a diversity of background social experience. For example, it has been shown that English public schools are staffed to a large extent by people who have themselves been public school pupils.[44] Equally, a university, a grammar school or a secondary modern school is staffed by people with relatively homogeneous backgrounds. Each of

[43] B. Wilson, 'The teacher's role; a sociological analysis', *British Journal of Sociology*, **13**, (1962).

[44] *cf.* G. Glennerster and R. Pryke, 'The Public Schools', *Young Fabian Pamphlet*, page 4 (1964).

these latter institutions will demand a certain kind of educational qualification and given the strong relationship between education received and social class,[45] this will mean that such staff are likely to share other social characteristics as well. Moreover, since schools and universities provide general rather than technical education, few of their teachers will have had occupational experience beyond the field of education which would have introduced some diversity among them. With regard to the area college,[46] some members of staff will have left school at fifteen years of age and any further education they may have acquired will have been the product of attendance at technical college evening classes or correspondence courses. At the other extreme there will be those who remained in full-time education until their mid-twenties as university students. With this variation in the amount of formal education received goes a difference in the kinds of educational qualifications possessed. Whereas some will have degrees in English and postgraduate degrees in science, for example, others will have certificates in engineering or shorthand and typing.

Not only are the staff of the area college characterised by such differences in educational backgrounds but also by a variety of occupational histories. At one extreme some will have entered the college immediately on graduation. At the other there will be those who have given up a career in school-teaching, personnel management or accountancy or who have been for a number of years on site work in the building industry or in an engineering workshop.

As we have said, the interesting question is what is the meaning of such diversity for the life of the college. March and Simon, for example, have suggested that

> 'the greater the homogeneity of background, the greater the extent of perceived goal-sharing'[47]

will be among members of an organisation. They have added, elsewhere, that

> 'An organisation that consists entirely of accountants has a great deal more homogeneity of individual goals than an organisation containing accountants, engineers, psychologists, and artists.'[48]

[45] cf. O. Banks, *The Sociology of Education,* London (1968), Chapter 3, part 3, pages 53–65, for a summary of the evidence.
[46] The following description is based on information obtained in interviews with Jones College teachers.
[47] J. G. March and H. A. Simon, *Organizations,* New York (1958), page 69.
[48] *Ibid.* page 125.

Certainly more than one writer has affirmed that the English public schools enjoys a high degree of consensus on values and goals.[49] However, before adopting a hypothesis incorporating a relationship between the area college's heterogeneity and goal conflict, it is important that consideration be given to the means by which an organisation, conceptually, could achieve a consensus.

There are probably three main ways in which similarities of outlook could occur among members of an organisation having diverse backgrounds. Firstly, it could be the result of an effective planned policy of orientation carried through by established members of the organisation or an agent. Secondly, it could be the product of the unplanned common experiences lived through by members of the organisation.[50] Thirdly, it is possible that, despite the ostensible diversity of their backgrounds, the individuals who opted to become members of the organisation did so because it stood for a purpose which was perceived commonly by them all and which they all wished to perpetuate in the same way.

In the educational field, the major form of planned orientation is the teacher training course. However, there is no compulsion on the new entrant to teaching in further education, to attend such a course and, as will be seen later,[51] few of the staff of Jones College were trained extensively, if at all.

Turning to the question of unplanned socialisation through the force of common experiences, the extent to which the staff of the area collage could be brought together in this way was not large. As we have indicated the college provided a great many courses for a variety of students: thus members of staff between them taught different subjects, at different levels, to different types of students, at different times of the day.[52]

Finally, to what extent was it possible that the college attracted to it those of like mind? This would depend partly upon the degree to which

[49] cf. R. Lambert, 'The Public Schools, a Sociological Introduction', in G. Kalton, *The Public Schools,* London (1966); J. Wilson, *Public Schools and Private Practice,* London (1962), Chapter 3; I. Weinberg, *The English Public Schools,* New York (1967), Chapter 3.

[50] cf. A. Etzioni, *A Comparative Analysis of Complex Organizations,* New York (1961), pages 141–149, for a discussion of planned and unplanned organisational socialisation.

[51] cf. Chapter 3.

[52] Members of Jones College staff who had previously worked in schools commented on the lack of the kind of communal tea, lunch and coffee breaks that existed in schools. This lack of concurrence was not merely because members of staff worked to different periods – evening class duties exempting staff from day-time ones – but also because not all departments worked to periods of the same timing. For example, the Engineering Department started at 9 a.m., the Business Studies Department at 9.15 a.m., and the Department of Catering at 9.30 a.m.

the college's image or character was clearly defined in society. It is instructive to consider Burton Clark's analysis of the American junior college in the process of considering this point.

The Problem of Organisational Identity

At the commencement of an investigation into a Californian junior college, Clark says,

> 'The junior college is a school whose place in education is by no means clear and whose character has been problematic. Not yet fixed in the American education system . . . the public junior college is more of an educational unknown than the elementary school, the high school, the private liberal arts college, the state college and the university.'[53]

The crisis of identity, according to Clark, stemmed from several factors. One was its administrative context. It was organised as part of the local school system, alongside elementary and high schools, yet its educational function was a post-school one and its enrolment figure and other statistics were actually included with those for higher education. Another was that the operation of an open-door admissions policy – that is allowing anyone to attend the college who wished to do so – brought the college a social cross-section of students. Thirdly, but a point that emanates from the second, the college had to accommodate disparate abilities and requirements: for instance, it had to provide vocational courses to prepare high school leavers for local industry and also general education courses for those who wished to enter senior colleges and universities ultimately.
The problem of the junior college, therefore, said Clark, was its diffuse commitments:

> 'Organisation character may vary greatly in degree of distinctiveness, which is generally gained by selective commitment and special symbols. A private college may combine a particular history of denominational support with a special constituency, take pride in specific campus buildings and noted graduates, and claim a type of undergraduate life not possessed by any other college. Above all, distinctive character is based on selective work and special competence.
> The emerging character of San José Junior College is relatively indistinct. Like most other public schools, its commitments are

[53] B. Clark, *The Open Door College,* New York (1960), page 2.

15

diffuse rather than selective. The college depends financially on the local tax-paying public and serves a broad-based clientele. Hence its social bases are diffuse compared to colleges that lean on more narrowly defined supports. As a public school, the college is expected to provide many kinds of services for many kinds of people . . .'[54]

In its administrative setting, the heterogeneity of its student population and the multi-purpose nature of its work, there is a striking parallel between the American junior college and the English area college. The latter too has probably an indistinct image in society. Certainly this was the impression of a sub-committee set up by the National Advisory Council on Education for Industry and Commerce. For in its report on 'The Public Relations of Further Education' it says:

'there is no doubt that the work of the colleges continues to be seriously handicapped by persistent ignorance and misunderstanding among young people, parents, schools, industry and the general public. In this respect there is a marked contrast between further education and the other main sectors of the educational system . . .'[55]

Moreover, in *Technical Education* a few years later there was an expression of concern about the erroneous image the public continued to hold of technical colleges:

'The idea of "night school" still persists, though evening class enrolments are the only figures in all education that are shrinking. But it is in the upper echelons that "the Tech" still needs to make its impact. It is still not sufficiently known that here is the second chance for the boy (or girl) who missed his Ordinary and Advanced levels at school, here is the way to a degree when entrance to a university is closed, here is the route to a professional qualification.'[56]

It seems unlikely that those members of our society who were to elect to join an area college as members of its staff would be any more capable

<hr />

[54] B. Clark, *op. cit.*, pages 142–143.

[55] A Report by a Sub-Committee of the National Advisory Council on Education for Industry and Commerce (1964), pages 6–7. Other reports made by official bodies have included comments on the complexity of the further education sector, for example, Ministry of Education, *Forward from School* (1962), page 70; Crowther Report, *op. cit.* para. 464, page 314.

[56] 'Ignorance of the "Tech" ', *Technical Education* (1966), page 248.

of formulating identical images of its purpose than the rest.[57] Having thus
accounted for the third means by which the heterogeneity of the
social background of Jones College staff might have been reduced in
significance, it follows that an important underlying hypothesis is that this
heterogeneity was likely to produce conflicts between staff over the
question of the goals of the college.

Research Techniques

It was not until some time after this research had commenced that
Eric Hoyle's article[58] was encountered, thus it was interesting to find
that the methodological approaches that he there recommends were
closely in line with those that we had in fact adopted. He suggests that
the researcher should make a choice from the following techniques: the
study of official documents, to understand the formal purpose of the
organisation; observation, especially at the stage of hypothesis formulation;
interviews, both unstructured and structured; questionnaires; and
historical study.[59]
As a researcher at Jones College whilst the project was in hand we were
in the position of observer. However, having been a technical college
teacher we have occupied the participant role as well, some of the time
at Jones itself.[60] Our association with the college spanned four years
in all. The problem of participant roles is that the researcher gains only
a segmental view of life in the organisation and so after having gathered
together some ideas through such means, we tended to rely more
upon other methods of data collection.
It was through interviews that most of our information on the climate of
interaction and staff attitudes was acquired. Relatively unstructured
interviews were held with those people who occupied unique positions in
the college, such as the Vice-Principal, the Registrar and Heads of
Departments. More structured interviews were held with full-time teaching
staff leaving the college at the end of the 1965–6 session. These interviews,
fifteen in number, served as a pilot scheme for the major set of interviews,

[57] Indeed, one or two members of staff, when asked during interviews whether
they were surprised by anything about the further education system on joining it,
remarked that they had been unaware of the diversity of the work that went on
in colleges.
[58] Hoyle, *op. cit.*
[59] *Ibid.* pages 108–109.
[60] Thus we moved between the various participant observer roles delimited by
Junker, namely those of complete participant, participant as observer,
observer as participant and complete observer. B. H. Junker, *Field Work.
An Introduction to the Social Sciences,* Chicago (1960).

17

those with a cross-section of the full-time teaching staff remaining with the college. The latter, fifty-seven in number, were conducted during the summer of the 1965–6 session and during the Autumn and Spring terms of the following session. Further details about the sampling procedure are to be found in Appendix IV.

The interviews rarely took less than two hours to complete and some were exceedingly protracted affairs. When possible the respondent was met at home, but on some occasions, and in all cases outside the major set of cross-sectional interviews, the interview took place in the college. The interviews were structured, but since the aim was to open a discussion, the questions were often of the open-ended kind and conversation was allowed to run on when it seemed that what was being said was important. The interviewing schedule is given in Appendix V. Because of the technique used, the reader will find that we have depended heavily upon the use of quotations from these discussions in presenting our material. We felt that it was only in this way that the 'feel' of the college could be conveyed.

The use of an historical approach and official documents was, of course, intrinsic to our particular task. We were fortunate in being given access to various college files, but there were always the documents that remained lost or secret.[61] We have described elsewhere the problems encountered when attempts to use educational statistics on an historical basis were made.[62]

[61] For example, it was not possible to scrutinise the minutes of meetings of the Board of Governors.

[62] cf. Chapter 3, page 31.

2. Official Policy and Technical College Goals

Jones College and other colleges were born of the stipulations in the 1944 Education Act about further education. However, the Act confined itself to two paragraphs on the subject of the nature of the further education that should be provided. The first of these runs as follows:

> 'Stages and purposes of statutory system of education. – The statutory system of public education shall be organised in three progressive stages to be known as primary education, secondary education, and further education; and it shall be the duty of the local education authority for every area, so far as their powers extend, to contribute towards the spiritual, moral, mental, and physical development of the community by securing that efficient education throughout those stages shall be available to meet the needs of the population of their area.'[1]

The second says:

> 'General duties of local education authorities with respect to further education. – . . . it shall be the duty of every local authority to secure the provision for their area of adequate facilities for further education, that is to say:
>
> (a) full-time and part-time education for persons over compulsory school age; and
> (b) leisure-time occupation, in such organised cultural training and recreation activities as are suited to their requirements, for any persons over compulsory school age who are able and willing to profit by the facilities provided for that purpose.'[2]

Thus the attitude towards the functions of further education could not have been more permissive whether with regard to the public it was to serve or the nature of the service that this public was to be provided with. (It should be noted, also, that local authorities were not required to satisfy all demands directly but were asked to 'secure provisions' only. This opened up the possibility of devolving some responsibility upon such other bodies as universities and the Workers Educational Association,[3] and thereby gave the local authority institutions a greater margin of choice than at first appears.) As we propose to show, subsequent official comment did little to clarify matters.

[1] The Education Act, 1944, part 2, section 7.
[2] *Ibid.* section 41.
[3] Indeed, part 2, section 42, paragraph 4 of the Act asks authorities to have regard for any facilities for further education already being provided by such bodies and to engage them in consultation.

Levels of Work in Colleges

The first major official comment after the Act on the emerging technical college structure was a White Paper issued in 1956[4] and a circular issued the same year elaborating on the proposals made in the White Paper.[5] The White Paper's main point was that a new type of college should be created specifically to provide advanced level courses, namely the college of advanced technology. The circular considers the relationships between the various types of colleges in the light of this proposal. It is in these documents that the nomenclature, local, area and regional colleges seems to appear for the first time, thereby indicating that some kind of pattern of colleges had emerged. This pattern has been described already.[6] The circular implies that having let colleges develop freely so far, it was time that the Ministry exercised some kind of control over their development. Three points are made about area colleges, our present concern. Firstly, their function of providing, in common with local colleges, non-advanced courses is described. No comment on this function is made and since elsewhere the circular is given to recommending adjustments, this lack of comment implies that no fault can be found with such a role.

The second point concerns part-time advanced work. Here the Ministry is more cautious and comes out against all area colleges developing such work:

> 'The Minister considers that the general aim, as far as Higher National Certificate and similar courses are concerned, should be to strengthen and expand the existing area colleges, where such courses are already provided.'[7]

The third point is a comment on full-time and sandwich-based advanced work:

> 'The Minister does not wish to disturb these arrangements so long as the courses remain efficent and economical, but . . . he thinks that the bulk of the new courses of these kinds should be provided at regional colleges or colleges of advanced technology.'[8]

From this it would seem reasonable to conclude that the official position on area colleges in the mid nineteen-fifties was that it was quite proper

[4] Ministry of Education, *Technical Education,* Cmnd. 9703 (1956).
[5] Ministry of Education, *The Organisation of Technical Colleges,* Circular 305.
[6] *cf.* Introduction, page 2.
[7] Circular 305, *op. cit.* paragraph 9, page 2.
[8] *Ibid.* paragraph 10, page 2.

for them to provide low level work but more advanced work was permissible for only a selected and existing number. However, elsewhere the circular casts doubt upon such a conclusion by seeming to suggest that it was perfectly legitimate for colleges to have upward mobility as one of their aims. At the beginning of the Circular is to be found the statement that:

> 'Within the regional pattern all colleges will be encouraged to expand the volume of their work and, when the circumstances justify it, to advance their status.'[9]

Whilst after having pronounced against the expansion of part-time advanced work beyond the existing establishments providing it and full-time advanced work beyond those courses already being run by area colleges, the circular goes on to add exceptional-case clauses for considering new applications for such work.

That the ladder principle was part of official policy becomes clear when another circular, issued five years later, is also examined.[10] This announced that regional colleges were about to be redesignated, and again the Ministry took pains not to appear inflexible. With regard to the list of colleges to be designated, the circular says:

> 'It is not the Minister's intention to fix the list of regional colleges once and for all time.'[11]

With regard to the policy of channelling advanced work into the regional colleges, it says:

> 'This has not precluded — and will not preclude in future — the approval of such courses at area colleges in the type of circumstances described in paragraph 10 of Circular 305.'[12]

Evidence for the conclusion that the Ministry had in fact allowed courses to continue to develop relatively freely is the report of the Committee on Technical College Resources which was published in 1966.[13] This stated that in the opinion of the Committee technical college resources were being wasted because courses were being run with too few students on them.

---

[9] Circular 305, *op. cit.* paragraph 4, page 1.
[10] Ministry of Education, *Regional Colleges,* Circular 3/61, 13th March (1961).
[11] *Ibid.* paragraph 14, page 4.
[12] Circular 3/61, *op. cit.* paragraph 3, page 2.
[13] *Report on the Size of Classes and Approval of Further Education Courses,* Committee on Technical College Resources, National Advisory Council on Education for Industry and Commerce, London (1966).

The Committee's recommendations, that new courses and new centres for courses should not be approved unless enrolments reached certain specified figures, were embodied in a circular issued in April, 1966.[14] This looked as if a clear criterion was being established once and for all : whether or not a course could be offered by a college was to depend upon enrolments. But the idea that clarity would immediately descend upon the situation was an illusion. Firstly, the specified enrolment figures for new courses were not without their exceptions. For example, in the case of full-time and sandwich students:

'(a) Experimental and other courses in novel or hitherto neglected fields: here the normal test should be whether the minimum annual enrolment will be attained within three years
(b) Courses in more specialised fields; it may be necessary to approve some courses of this nature where demand is never likely to reach the minimum
(c) Courses where physical limitations of space restrict the numbers it is practicable to enrol'.[15]

And other considerations included whether or not students could attend alternative courses within 'reasonable travelling distance'.
Secondly, there was the problem of existing courses:

'All existing courses should be reviewed in the light of these new criteria. It may be right to allow such courses to continue for a time without full enrolments until the resources, of both staff and accommodation, already committed can be otherwise employed. Special consideration should also be given to courses with low enrolments where it is known that the figure normally required will be reached within a year or two'.[16]

The situation, therefore, was still confused.
Following close on the heels of the report on the Size of Classes was the publication of a White Paper, 'A Plan for Polytechnics and Other Colleges'.[17] This proposed that a limited number of colleges should be designated 'Polytechnics' with the object of building up a strong sector of higher education complementary to the universities and colleges of education. It was in these colleges, additions to which were not intended

[14] Department of Education and Science, *Technical College Resources: Size of Classes and Approval of Further Education Courses,* Circular 11/66, 12 April (1966).
[15] Circular 11/66, *op. cit.* Appendix, section 3.
[16] *Ibid.* section 4.
[17] Department of Education and Science, *A Plan for Polytechnics and Other Colleges, op. cit.*

to be made for about ten years, that the technical college system's full-time and sandwich higher education was to be concentrated.

Once again, however, the door was not altogether closed in the faces of other colleges. The Polytechnics were not to be allowed to have a monopoly of full-time higher education in the further education sector, says the White Paper:

> 'Their work will need to be supplemented by that of many other colleges, particularly in specialist fields . . . Full-time courses of higher education in specific professional fields such as art, architecture, agriculture, social work, management studies, nautical studies, institutional management and catering . . . will continue if the need for them can be established in terms of current criteria for the approval of courses.'[18]

And full-time higher education must also continue, adds the White Paper, where there are special needs which neither polytechnics nor the specialist centres can meet.[19]

With regard to part-time higher education, the White Paper, while stressing the need for its concentration as far as possible in selected centres, recommended that colleges already engaged in such work should continue to do so so long as they were able to satisfy the criteria for course approval currently in force.[20]

Breadth of Work in Colleges

The 1944 Education Act made local authorities responsible for securing the provision of 'education' and 'cultural training and recreation' for those over compulsory school age. But whether the education should be general or vocational and what kinds of cultural and recreational activities it was proper for public money to be spent upon were questions the Act did not pursue. Subsequently more detailed recommendations came down to authorities and colleges in circulars and administrative memoranda, but these merely exhorted them to carry out a miscellany of activities and were of little help with the problem of making choices and defining tasks. A selection from these communications will be given to illustrate their diversity.

The Act coincided with the ending of the second world war, and for the years immediately after it colleges were called upon to play a part in the

---

[18] *A Plan for Polytechnics and Other Colleges, op. cit.* paragraphs 19–20, page 7.
[19] *Ibid.* paragraph 22, page 7.
[20] *A Plan for Polytechnics and Other Colleges, op. cit.* paragraph 23, page 8.

post-war reconstruction drive, both with respect to the provision of training facilities,

> 'As demobilisation proceeds, technical colleges will be expected to play their part in the provision of full-time training at the Government's expense under the Resettlement Scheme of the Ministry of Labour and National Service . . .
> The provision of further training facilities for the building industry . . . is a very urgent matter.'[21]

and by contributing to the advancement of knowledge,

> 'Today it is more than ever important . . . to ensure that scientific and technical research is carried out as widely and intensively as possible and applied promptly to production . . .'[22]

At the same time, a circular was sent out to colleges about homecraft:

> 'An incalculable sum of human happiness and efficiency depends upon the knowledge and skill applied to the running of the home and the upbringing of children . . . The further education service must help to build them up by providing instruction in homecraft for housewives and mothers of the future.'[23]

One noticeable element in the recommendations of the nineteen-fifties was the requests to colleges to contribute towards scientific and technological education and training, and to the supply of technicians.[24] Another was the movement to liberalise technical courses.[25] Although not entirely neglected previously, the nineteen-sixties were marked by the attention that was given to management and allied studies. As a consequence of a report by the Advisory Committee on Further Education for Commerce in 1959, it was announced that commercial

[21] Ministry of Education, *Further Education – Some Immediate Problems,* Circular 56, 9 July (1945).
[22] Ministry of Education, *Research in Technical Colleges,* Circular 94, 8 April (1946).
[23] Ministry of Education, *Further Education Homecraft,* Circular 117, 5 July (1946). Other examples to illustrate the diversity of recommendations being made in this period could have been given, *cf.* Ministry of Education, *Training for the Catering Industry,* Circular 109, 23 May (1946).
[24] *cf.,* for example, Ministry of Education, *Advanced Short Courses for Scientists and Technologists Engaged in Industry, Circular 270,* 27 August (1953); Ministry of Education, *Technical Education, op. cit.* These requests were backed up with the provision of a special Advanced Technology Grant in 1952 for authorities providing higher technological education, *cf.* Ministry of Education, *Advanced Technology,* Circular 255, 14 July (1952).
[25] *cf.* Ministry of Education, *Liberal Education in Technical Colleges,* Circular 323, 13 May (1957).

education would get a special measure of priority in the building programmes for 1962–3 and the following year.[26] One other result of this report, although the decision was made with an eye to the needs of management education also, was the establishment of a new Higher National Diploma in Business Studies, to run from September 1962.[27] In 1959 the Ministry also received a report from a Working Party set up by the Joint (Examinations) Executive Committee for Management Studies and this resulted in the establishment of a revised Diploma in Management in 1961, an award designed to mark the completion of a a course in advanced management.[28]

The first report of the United Kingdom Advisory Council on Education for Management, published in December 1962, dealt in particular with the progress of the Diploma in Management, and a circular issued the following year, taking its cue from the Council, urged colleges to make greater efforts to expand this work.[29] The Council's second report, published in January 1966, commented upon provisions that colleges should offer in addition to the Diploma work, and these recommendations were taken up by the Department of Education with similar alacrity and put into Circular 2/66:

> 'The Secretary of State shares the belief of the Council that the technical colleges should be able to make an important contribution to the needs of functional management.'[30]

At the same time as colleges were being asked to play an increasing part in the field of management education and training, their attention was being drawn to the vocational and non-vocational needs of school leavers and young workers. In 1959 the Crowther Report on the education of boys and girls between the ages of 15 and 18 was published[31] and this was followed by a White Paper,[32] an administrative memorandum[33]

[26] cf. Ministry of Education, *Technical Education – The Next Step,* Circular 1/59, 13 April (1959); Ministry of Education, *Further Education for Commerce,* Circular 5/59, 11 June (1959).

[27] cf. Circular 5/59, *op. cit.;* Ministry of Education, *The Future Development of Management Education and of Business Studies,* Circular 1/60, 28 March (1960); Ministry of Education, *National Certificates and Diplomas in Business Studies,* Administrative Memorandum 7/61, Addendum 1, 15 February (1962).

[28] cf. Circular 1/60, *op. cit.*

[29] Ministry of Education, *Management Education,* Circular 7/63, 7 May (1963).

[30] Department of Education and Science, *Management Studies in Technical Colleges,* Circular 2/66, 10 January (1966).

[31] Report of the Central Advisory Council for Education, *op. cit.*

[32] Ministry of Education, *Better Opportunities in Technical Education,* Cmnd. 1254 (1961).

[33] Ministry of Education, *Forward from School,* Administrative Memorandum 6/62, 17 May (1962).

and a circular,[34] all devoted to the topic of the establishment of continuity between schools and further education and the education of the young worker. The 1964 Industrial Training Act strengthened this emphasis.[35] The same year, the Henniker-Heaton Committee reported on day release for young people under the age of 18. Circular 14/64 passes on to local authorities the Committee's recommendation that they, directly or through their colleges, should launch a sustained campaign to expand day release on a voluntary basis.[36]

Conclusion

The 1944 Education Act laid down the functions of the further education system in extremely vague terms. Although subsequent official communications supplied a certain amount of detail, they did little to clarify for the individual college what its overall goals should be and where its priorities ought to lie in the face of limitations on meeting them.
The position of the area college was particularly confusing. With regard to the standard of work it should pursue, the situation changed from one in which the field was completely open, to one of ambiguity. Having the title of area college, it appeared to have some kind of right to go beyond the low level work that was the province of the local college. Yet whether it ought to pursue advanced work, and if so to what extent, was far from clear. The breadth of the field with which it was confronted was vast, and quite clearly it would have been impossible for any one college to have put into practice all the recommendations made to it. Yet these recommendations appeared to be made in a completely disconnected fashion unaccompanied by any advice to colleges about priorities. Etzioni has said that the goals of an organisation

> 'provide orientation by depicting a future state of affairs which the organisation strives to realise. Thus they set down guide lines for organisational activity. Goals also constitute a source of legitimation which justifies the activities of an organisation and, indeed, its very existence.'[37]

In terms of its logic, this statement sounds sensible: one can envisage

[34] Ministry of Education, *Organisation of Further Education Courses,* Circular 3/63, 18 February (1963).

[35] *cf.* Department of Education and Science, *The Industrial Training Act, 1964,* Administrative Memorandum 4/64, 23 April (1964).

[36] Department of Education and Science, *The Henniker-Heaton Report on Day Release,* Circular 14/64, 6 October (1964).

[37] A. Etzioni, *Modern Organisations,* New Jersey (1964), page 5.

clear official goals acting in such a way. But more useful to us is the opposite train of thought it encourages. As we have seen, the official goals for the area college were not clear, thus guidelines were weak. This would put into the hands of the members of the college and those responsible for it – that is, the Board of Governors and the Local Education Committee – the job of deciding what it should actually do. And because the official goals were vague, there were plenty of grounds on which activities actually pursued, or mooted, could be justified if necessary: but equally, those who objected to certain activities stood a considerable chance of finding grounds on which to support their objections.

It makes a useful preamble to the case-study to follow to mention what may have been the most profound disagreement about policy that ever occurred among the Governors of Jones College and the Local Authority's Education Committee.[38] The controversy that we are referring to arose over the Department of Education's Polytechnic Plan and the suggestion in the White Paper that Polytechnic status might be acquired by the merging of colleges. The issue was whether or not Jones College should merge with two other area colleges for this purpose. If it did not make such a move, maintained some members of the Education Committee, then the chances were that Jones College would eventually lose the advanced work that it currently possessed. If a merger did come about, said other members, more than 12 000 students studying below Polytechnic level at the college would be without provisions.[39] The Education Committee finally approved a merger plan but not, according to the newspaper reports, without strong protests. A fortnight later, however, the plan was rejected by the Department. An interesting point was that this dispute did not rest at the level of the Education Committee. A number of its members were also Governors of the college and indeed one of the strongest advocates for the merger in the Committee and the most vocal member of the Committee against it were the Chairman and Vice-Chairman of the Governors respectively.

[38] These events were reported in the local press between 23 March and 14 April 1967.
[39] The local press, which normally confined its coverage of the college to the occasional mention of a social event, usually in small type, contained headlines such as *Intellectual Elite or Trained Technicians and Craftsmen?* and *Protests at 'Poly-Plan' for Jones College.*

PART 2

3 Jones College, Its Setting and Development

The first mention of a plan for a college on the site now occupied by
Jones College is to be found in the county's 'Scheme for Education and
Plan for County Colleges' published in draft form in December 1948.
The background to this document is Part 2[1] of the 1944 Education Act,
which made it the duty of every local education authority to prepare such
schemes when so directed by the Minister, and Circulars 133 and 139[2]
sent out three years later giving 1948 as the deadline for the submission
of the schemes.
The 'Scheme for Education' shows that for the particular area of the
county with which we are concerned[3] it was proposed that there should
be a Central College of Further Education and three County Colleges.
The County College plan – compulsory release from work for young
people to attend colleges – was not put into practice and the three latter
colleges came to nought, but a college for further education did materialise.
It was established in 1951 in the buildings and huts newly vacated by a
technical school which had moved to another site.[4] In the same year a
schedule of accommodation for a new college was prepared and in
April 1954 the construction of new buildings and demolition of the old
ones on the site began.[5] In 1967 additional buildings were still going up
although these were said to be the last that the site could take.
Geographically, Jones College was situated in the south of England. Its
administrative catchment area, designated to it in the 1948 Plan, contained
the municipal borough within which it stood, with a population of just
under 81 000 at the 1961 Census, an adjacent urban district with a
population of 4000, and a rural district with a population of 27 000.
However, an attempt to define the college's catchment area is bedevilled
by two things: one is that the county boundaries at this point of the
country were such that parts of the neighbouring counties were as near
to the college as parts of its own administrative area. The other is that the
region had first-class road and main-line rail links with other parts of the
country. In this situation the geographical relationship of the college with
other establishments of further and higher education becomes important.

[1] The 1944 Education Act, Part 2, Sections 42 and 43.
[2] Ministry of Education, *Schemes of Further Education and Plans for County
Colleges,* Circular 133, 19 March (1947) and *Plans for County Colleges,*
Circular 139, 3 April (1947).
[3] The county was divided into 5 areas and further education provisions were
made for each of these individually.
[4] Verbal information from the Vice-Principal.
[5] Information from a set of notes compiled by the college for a visit of
Her Majesty's Inspectors in 1961.

Within a radius of fifteen miles there were three other colleges of Area standard,[6] one of these belonging to the same local education authority as Jones College but standing in the adjoining administrative area, the others belonging to the neighbouring county authorities. Local colleges existed near to Jones College but none of these came within its area and indeed the nearest one, three miles to the south, belonged to a different authority entirely. Within a twenty-one mile radius there were three universities. In addition to all of this, much of the London further education system was within reach without too much effort.

Jones College's strength in the face of this highly competitive situation lay in the fact that it had on its doorstep a flourishing industrial complex. As at May 1964,[7] the number working in the borough alone was well over 60 000, and a *Guardian* reporter describing the scene in October 1965 said there were 'Seven jobs vacant for every two men and thirteen for every woman'. The industries represented were varied but tended to be light. The six largest were engineering and electrical goods (13 303), chemicals (7471), food, drink and tobacco (5824), distribution (4253), metal manufacture (3809) and miscellaneous services (3804).[8] Probably the best available summary of the character of the place is that made by a *Times* newspaper correspondent analysing constituencies prior to the 1964 General Election. He describes the 'Jones' constituency as follows:

> 'For the Martian sociologist with a limited season return spaceship ticket, Jones is instant Britain, 1964. Slice the constituency at any point and there is revealed the whole country in all its splendour, in all its malaise. Jones, the cynics would say, has everything and yet has nothing . . .
>
> Along the main road the supermarkets stand shoulder to shoulder, yelling their cut-price messages from posters in phosphorous reds and greens. The television, washing-machine, veneered cocktail cabinet status symbols leer from their plate-glass lairs.
>
> The well-fed, well-dressed, passers-by worrying their way along the packed pavements and through the thundering traffic, gaze back, only half-seeing, while big jets claw their way deafeningly into the sky overhead.

[6] A letter from the Department of Education and Science, in reply to the author's enquiry, stated that no index of the status of individual technical colleges existed. Here a status has been ascribed to a college after perusal of its prospectus.

[7] Information supplied by the Manager of the local branch of the Ministry of Labour.

[8] *Ibid.*

But Jones has more ingredients in the contemporary boiling even than these. It has overspill from London; . . . unskilled repetition produces wages undreamed of a decade ago; it has 1000 unfilled jobs; it has 5000 coloured immigrants.'

A Note on Further Education Statistics

A word of explanation about the statistical data that follows is called for. Two problems in particular were encountered in the search for statistical information. One was that some kinds of data had been collected only in recent years or was not collected at all – an example of the latter was the job destinations of staff resigning their appointments with the college. The other was that there had been very little conscious effort made on the part of the college office to keep material once it had served its purpose in furnishing returns called for by the local and central education authorities. Thus the statistical information that follows is the product of much probing among old correspondence, prospectuses, registers and minutes of various kinds that had managed to escape the wastepaper basket. It is interesting, therefore, to find that W. D. Wall, talking on research in the field of further education at the 1966 National Education Conference, should say that:

'one of the major problems was in fact the simplest one to solve – the almost incredible anarchy in college record-keeping, the lack of elementary statistical information on technical colleges'.[9]

Because data has been obtained in this piece-meal fashion it has been difficult to avoid allowing certain discrepancies and discontinuities to remain among the figures that follow.

Growth and Change

As can be seen from Table 1, between 1951–2 and 1965–6 the number of students enrolled at Jones College increased five-fold. A slight contraction took place the following year, the reason for which will emerge later on. In terms of student hours, a better index of the college's actual work load, the growth rate was even larger, of course. This can be seen in Appendix I. Table 1 tells us more than this, however, for it shows that from being an institution devoted primarily to the teaching of

[9] W. D. Wall, 'Educational Research in Technical Colleges', a paper given to the 1966 National Educational Conferences, Further Education Section.

evening class students, the college, by 1966, had become rather more involved with part-time day students than evenings-only students and in addition had acquired a substantial body of full-time and sandwich students. In terms of its work load this structural transition is even more noticeable as Table 2 shows.

Table 1. Student Enrolments

Year	Full-time	Sand-wich	Short Courses	Part-time Day	Evenings only	Total	Growth Rate
			*				
1951–2	8	—	—	812	1973	2793	100·0
1952–3	47	—	—	907	2168	3122	111·8
1953–4	81	—	—	1020	2292	3393	121·5
1954–5	87	—	—	1141	2644	3872	138·6
1955–6	114	—	—	1348	3202	4664	167·0
1956–7	147	—	—	1678	3206	5031	180·1
1957–8	189	—	—	1914	3912 (1503) †	6015	215·4
1958–9	251	—	(560)‡	2037	4207 (1533)	6495	232·5
1959–0	349	19	—	2191	4881 (1496)	7441	266·4
1960–1	370	28	—	3111 (479) †	4743 (837)	8256	295·6
1961–2	401	32	1065	3370 (649)	4736 (677)	9604	343·9
1962–3	394	46	845	3736 (680)	5631 (886)	10 652	381·4
1963–4	499	78	1354	4530 (868)	6027 (899)	12 488	447·1
1964–5	561	120	1392	4937 (736)	5451 (682)	12 461	446·2
1965–6	586	195	1341	5701 (1181)	5983 (695)	13 806	494·3
1966–7	658	253	805	5676 (481)	4712 (275)	12 104	433·4

Sources: College copies of Ministry of Education, Returns for Major Establishments of Further Education, Form 13E, for years 1951–2 to 1956–7. College monthly enrolments, General Office records, and County Education Committee, Statistics for Further Education, for years 1957–8 onwards. Miscellaneous general office files.

* Where no figures occur in this column it must be assumed that the enrolments have been included in those of other columns according to the basis of the short course, full-time, evening, etc. However, it is uncertain when the college began to run short courses.

† Figures in brackets represent students attending classes run in surrounding centres administered by the college. Prior to 1960–1 they were all classified as evening students although many of the classes were in fact held in the day-time. No separate classification for this group of students can be found for the earlier period.

‡ These short courses are included in the other columns.

Because of statistical adjustments the years 1951 and 1966 are not fully comparable, as the notes to Table 2 explain. However, by looking at the periods 1951–2 to 1956–7 and 1961–2 and 1966–7 separately the trend can be observed.

Table 2. Distribution of Student Hours between Types of Courses

Percentages of total hours

	1951–2	1956–7	1961–2	1966–7
Evening *	49·8	39·6	24·6	16·6
Part-time day†	48·5	39·5	42·9	43·9
Full-time	1·7	20·9	30·8	30·1
Sandwich	—	—	1·7	9·1
Short courses	—	—	—	0·3
	100·0	100·0	100·0	100·0

Source: Appendix I.

* 1951–2 and 1956–7 include evening classes attended by day students and day attendance in detached centres. But these are excluded thereafter.

† 1951–2 and 1956–7 exclude evening classes attended by day students and day attendance in detached centres, but these are included thereafter.

Table 3. Levels of Work

In student hours

Levels *	1951–2		1956–7		1961–2		1966–7	
	Number	%	Number	%	Number	%	Number	%
University	4088	1·5	60 928	8·9	162 080	12·6	598 574	30·6
Upper Advanced	72 837	26·2	222 909	32·6	217 645	16·9	483 075	24·7
Lower Advanced					235 912	10·3	436 066	22·3
School	201 010	72·3	400 694	58·5	671 333	52·2	437 102	22·4
	277 935	100·0	684 531	100·0	1 286 970	100·0	1 954 706	100·0

Source: College copy of Ministry of Education, Returns for Major Establishments of Further Education, Form 6K, for year 1951–2. College returns to County Education Committee for 1956–7, 1961–2 and 1966–7.

* The bases of these classifications were the General Certificate of Education and the National Certificates, other qualifications being looked at in the light of these. Thus an HND course constituted 'university' level work, the second year of a GCE Advanced level course or an OND course 'upper advanced' work and the first year of of these courses 'lower advanced' work. 'School' level work thus included GCE Ordinary level courses. (Information supplied by the College Clerk.)

The next aspect of the college's development to be examined is its standard of work. In 1951, three categories were used in analysing this: in 1959, the middle category, 'advanced' work, was split into upper and lower advanced work. Definitions of these categories will be found in a note to Table 3 which sets out this development. As the table shows, a quite drastic change took place during fifteen years. However, a certain amount of caution is necessary in the interpretation of these figures since the assignment of a course to a category is not always a straightforward process. In the case of a course lacking an easily definable academic content, its assignment will depend upon the judgment of a General Office clerk and the relevant Head of Department; and in the last analysis, where these cannot agree, the Principal.[10] However, the clerk concerned said, 'It is very difficult for Heads of Departments to acknowledge that their courses are lower levels.'

One way in which the college's development in breadth can be observed is in its changing departmental structure. The 1951–2 Prospectus gives no indication that the college had been arranged on a departmental basis, but from the Prospectus of the following year it is possible to see that, by then, three existed, namely a Department of Engineering and Building, a Department of Science and a Department of Commerce and General Education. A process of departmental bifurcation, changes of nomenclature and the establishment of completely new departments followed. In 1953, a Department of Domestic Studies and Catering was added, the Engineering and Building Department split into two self-contained units in 1956, and by 1958 the Commerce and General Education Department had had the term 'Management' incorporated into its title. Four years later, the latter was reorganised into two separate units as the Department of General Studies and the Department of Management and Business Studies. It was planned that for the 1967–8 session the latter would be divided into a Department of Management and a Department of Professional and Business Studies and that a Department of Mathematics and Computing would be newly established. By then there would be eight departments in all.

One feature of the departmental structure was the imbalance of these departments in terms of both the quality of their work and their size. Tables 4 and 5 illustrate this. Particularly noticeable is the quick rise of the Management Department to a dominant position in both terms.

Our final index of growth is staff expansion. Membership of the full-time teaching staff increased from 13 to 238 between 1951–2 and 1966–7, the number of part-time teachers increasing from 143 to 378 between 1951–2

[10] Information supplied by the college's general office.

Table 4. Distribution of Work Between Departments by Quantity

In student hours

Department	1956–7		1961–2		1966–7	
	Number	%	Number	%	Number	%
Engineering	225 349	34·5	336 856	27·1	402 296	20·8
Building	43 305	6·6	64 077	5·2	126 673	6·5
Science	71 305	10·9	168 856	13·6	183 179	9·5
Management and Business Studies	—	—	243 898*	19·6	599 186	30·9
General Studies	242 381	37·1	220 261*	17·7	338 884	17·5
Catering, Fashion and Home Economics	71 546	10·9	207 528	16·7	286 701	14·8
Total†	653 886	100·0	1 241 476	100·0	1 936 919	100·0

Source: Calculated from College returns to County Education Committee.
 * Statistics collected separately although departments not divided until the following year.
 † These totals differ from those in Appendix I as figures for the detached centres have been omitted.

and 1964–5. Clerical and administrative workers in the college went up from 7 to 34 between 1958–9 and 1966–7, and over the same period the number of technicians went up from 14 to 58.

Thus, over the period 1951 to 1966, Jones College experienced considerable growth and change. One member of staff who had taught at the college since its early days summarised its growth when he said, 'It was very pleasant when all the people who stayed for lunch could sit round one table.' In character it had changed from an institution working preponderantly at a junior level to one which classified almost one-third of its work as 'university' level and under one-quarter as 'school' level. It had changed also from an institution where the great majority of its students attended on an evenings-only basis to one where the number of part-time day students outstripped those on evenings-only courses and which had over 900 students attending full-time or sandwich courses. (Moreover, in terms of the volume of work, the latter took up 40% of the total student hours in 1966–7.)

Table 5. Distribution of Work Between Departments by Quality

Student hours, in percentages

Levels of work by Departments	Importance of level of work within Departments		Departmental contribution to each level of total college work	
	1956–7	1966–7	1956–7	1966–7
University				
Engineering	13·3	28·3	49·3	19·0
Building	3·5	22·7	2·5	4·8
Science	24·0	54·3	28·1	16·6
Management, etc.	—	53·9	—	53·9
General Studies	5·1	6·1	2·02	3·4
Catering, etc.	—	4·6	— (100%)	2·2(100%)
Upper Advanced				
Engineering	36·6	22·9	38·2	19·1
Building	25·8	18·7	4·9	4·9
Science	27·8	29·3	18·2	10·9
Management, etc.	—	30·0	—	37·3
General Studies	23·9	18·0	25·5	12·6
Catering, etc.	41·8	25·3	13·2(100%)	15·0(100%)
Lower Advanced				
Engineering		24·7		22·8
Building		22·8		6·6
Science		5·7		6·6
Management, etc.		11·8		16·3
General Studies		20·8		16·2
Catering, etc.		48·0		31·6(100%)
School Level				
Engineering	50·1(100%)	24·1(100%)	30·5	23·1
Building	70·7(100%)	35·8(100%)	8·3	10·8
Science	18·2(100%)	0·7(100%)	3·5	0·3
Management, etc.	— (100%)	4·3(100%)	—	6·1
General Studies	71·0(100%)	55·1(100%)	46·5	44·5
Catering, etc.	58·2(100%)	22·1(100%)	11·2(100%)	15·2(100%)

Source: Calculated from returns to County Education Committee.

The Changes Analysed

Were these developments the result of spontaneous responses to demands from firms, schools and individuals on the part of the college? Were they the result of attempts to put into action Government policy? What part did members of the college play in determining the course of the college's

development? No precise answers can be given to such questions, but
it is evident that the college followed neither the force of demand
nor the spirit of recommendations embodied in official policy documents
altogether.

(a) *The Demand Available*

According to the 1961 Census, the county in which Jones College was
situated was among the fastest-growing counties in England and Wales
between 1951 and 1961. The annual increase in population over this
period for the country as a whole was 0·5 per cent; that for the county
with which we are concerned was well over 2·25 per cent. Moreover, the
municipal borough within which Jones College was situated was the
fastest growing of the county's boroughs (registering an increase of
more than 14 000) and its adjacent rural district was the fastest growing
rural district in the county (registering an increase of nearly 24 000). Had
the county's growth been the result simply of an excess of births over
deaths then it would have had no significance for further education for that
period. However, according to the Census, 'a little under three-quarters
of this increase was due to the inward movement of population'. This
population expansion coupled with its related feature, the economic
buoyancy of the area, would lead one to expect a higher than average
growth rate at Jones College. In Appendix II is given, though very
tentatively because of the statistical problems involved, a comparison
between Jones College and similar institutions in the country as a whole,
and from this it appears that Jones College's rate of growth was
ahead of the national one.[11]

Nevertheless, it is clear that the college did not proceed merely to attempt
to satisfy the most readily available demand.

In the Principal's report to a meeting of the Engineering Advisory
Committee[12] in November, 1964, there is a reference to the transfer of
part-time day students from Jones College to a college in the
adjoining county:

> 'This Session . . . College was able to accommodate the whole of
> the first year of the Mechanical Engineering Craft Practice course.'

[11] It was not possible to compare the growth rate of Jones College with that for
area colleges as a whole, which would have constituted a more meaningful comparison,
because the statistics contained insufficiently fine breakdowns. The second
footnote to Appendix II enlarges on this point.

[12] Each of the college's departments, except the General Studies Department, had
an advisory committee composed of representatives of local firms and organisations,
the local authority's Education Committee and the Governors. Their meetings were
attended also by the Principal and the appropriate Head of Department.

The minutes of that meeting show that later on the topic was returned to:

> 'The Principal said that the arrangements whereby some of our students were being accommodated at the . . . College was in line with plans agreed some time ago between the two educational authorities . . . the agreement was for . . . College to take up to 800 part-time students of all types for about 3 years until the new . . . College was ready.'

(The 'new' college in this quotation is a reference to a plan for a local college which would come under the jurisdiction of the same authority as Jones College and take over its junior work. However, even by 1967, there had been no final decision taken about this project despite the impression given in the above remark that actual building was in progress.) The Commerce Advisory Committee was listening to similar proposals in May 1965, from the Principal concerning the Department of Management and Business Studies:

> 'It is proposed to *continue*[13] to transfer certain courses to . . . College in 1965/6.'

The courses referred to in this instance were full-time commercial courses, part-time copy-typing courses and part-time courses leading to the Certificate in Office Studies.

From the 1964–5 session onwards, Jones College courses were also being filtered into new Evening Institutions.[14] In this case the work was that for which the Department of General Studies had had responsibility, such as GCE Ordinary level courses[15] and recreational classes.[16] The impact of this policy can be judged from the decline in the figures for evening class enrolments in Table 1.

Was the explanation for this policy of transferring work elsewhere overcrowding? Certainly, over the period that we were directly involved with the work of the college, space was at a premium. Classes were held in hired accommodation at inconvenient distances from the college; for example, one centre was a bus ride away and the bus service was not always good. Or they were held on parts of the college premises not designed for such purposes, for example, in windowless rooms behind

---

[13] Author's italics.

[14] *cf.* Minutes of a Heads of Departments Meeting, 11 May (1964).

[15] The General Studies Department was responsible for all the GCE Ordinary level work in the college.

[16] Woodwork, Cake Icing and Preliminary Music courses are three examples of recreational courses that the 1966–7 Prospectus announced would be held in Evening Institutes.

the stage intended as dressing and prop rooms. Moreover, the documents reveal that the situation of overcrowding was endemic.[17] However, at the same time as some courses were being thus removed from the college, effort was being expended upon persuading the market and official bodies to support its running of others.

(b) The Demand Wanted

As will have been noticed no doubt, the work that was being transferred was junior level work, basic craft and office training, elementary general education and recreational courses. The work that the college sought was of a more advanced type.

The enthusiasm for advanced work can be seen from the following comments made by two heads of departments during our interviews with them. In reply to a question which asked whether the decision to remove the craft courses from Jones College was a local authority or a college decision, one head of department said:

> 'It was a college decision on the grounds of limited accommodation and the fact that we have advanced equipment which should be used for advanced training rather than basic training. At least, these were the admitted reasons. The other one, which was never given outright, was that because we were going for CNAA[18] we did not wish to go for low level work.'

Asked about his views on the desirability of short courses, the same man replied:

> 'Short courses are advanced work. Therefore they enhance the reputation of the department and the college.'

Asked the same question about short courses, the other head of department voiced similar sentiments.

> 'I think they are very desirable and I am trying to build them up. This is tactical. If I can run them I can build up the status of the department because they are rated more highly . . . I could easily pack the department with more Ordinary levels, for instance. This would be a very simple thing to do since it is easy to get students because no pre-requisite qualifications are required of applicants.'

---

[17] 'The Principal reported that consideration was being given to a proposal to erect seven huts to provide temporary accommodation.' (Minutes of a Heads of Department Meeting, 12 January 1959.) 'The Science Department was proposing to stagger classes in order to utilise laboratories more fully and the Principal asked other Departments to consider similar possibilities.' (*op. cit.* 19 October, 1959.)

[18] *cf.* page 42.

Whilst a third head of department made his feelings plain during an address to a departmental staff meeting:

> 'I want to make this the best . . . Department in the country. Last year student hours increased enormously, and all at what the Ministry calls university level work. And that's the only description of our work I like to consider ourselves doing.'

The documents particularly provided us with a considerable amount of information on the effort expended on building up advanced work in the college over the years. Repeatedly we see that the college had to battle with the authorities, with the market and with other colleges either for permission to run courses or to get them supported. Firstly let us look at the full-time and sandwich advanced courses.

As early as November 1956 the Principal was telling the Engineering Advisory Committee that he was concerned about the lack of definite support for a proposed full-time Senior Engineering Course.[19] Whilst at the same meeting a member of the committee proffered the information that his firm had received an enquiry from another technical college about a sandwich course in mechanical engineering that had been proposed for Jones College. The latter course turned out to be quite a perennial problem, for although an HND Mechanical Engineering course was eventually started in the 1958–9 session, the Principal was found to be reporting to the Committee in the May that

> 'he had hoped to see, after the beginning of that course, increased interest on the part of local firms, but the present position was that there had been no extension of the list of firms supporting the course'.[20]

And in November 1962, he was expressing anxiety about the possibility that a neighbouring college would be applying for recognition for the same course. Since the course at Jones College was only just meeting Ministry requirements, he was reported as saying, such a move by the neighbouring college was likely to have implications for Jones College.[21] Rivalry of this kind occurred over an HND Electrical Engineering course as well. The Committee in November 1963 was told by the Principal that on the basis of a survey among local firms it appeared the support for such a course would be meagre.[22] Nevertheless, the college must have gone ahead and submitted a proposal for the course

[19] cf. Minutes of an Engineering Advisory Committee meeting, 20 November (1956).
[20] Ibid. 14 May (1959).
[21] Ibid. 13 November (1962).
[22] Ibid. 5 November (1963).

to the Department of Education and Science, because two years later
the Committee was being informed by the Principal that such a proposal
had been rejected.[23] Apparently the college had been invited to re-submit
it for the 1966–7 session, but the matter was not a straightforward one
between Jones College and the Department as the following extract from
the Principal's same Report indicates:

'since . . . College had also submitted a similar scheme, it was
now a matter for discussion between the Principals of the two
Colleges and the Department of Education and Science'.

The course did not run at Jones College in the 1966–7 session.
From the minutes of meetings of the Science Advisory Committee it can
be seen that the Science Department was involved in making similar
plans and encountering similar difficulties. A minute of a November 1959
meeting contains the following general statement:

'A discussion took place on the difficulty that had been
experienced by the college in pursuing its plans for developing
advanced science courses.'

And more specifically it goes on to report that the Ministry of Education
had been unable to support a proposal for a full-time course leading to
Graduateship of the Royal Institute of Chemistry. This support was
eventually forthcoming, it seems, but the tardiness of it was proved
justified, for in November 1963 we find the Principal reporting to the
Committee that Part II of the course had had to be cancelled for lack
of enrolments.
The minutes of a May 1964 meeting illustrate, once again, the Science
Department's market problems in this field of advanced courses, and this
time the college's relationship with other institutions is made plain
also. The minutes report that the college had been approved to run a
full-time B.Sc. (General) degree course in Chemistry, Physics and
Mathematics, subject to its attaining a minimum enrolment of 25 students
for the first year of the course. Members of the Committee, however, felt
that

'it would be impossible to secure such a number for the three subjects
named and suggested that many students would prefer Statistics
as an alternative subject to Chemistry and many more would prefer
Biology. The requirement for entry to the course would in effect be
Advanced level passes in all three subjects, and students with
such a qualification would certainly be accepted by a University.

[23] Minutes of an Engineering Advisory Committee Meeting, 20 November (1956).

41

Already other colleges were canvassing for students for their courses with a full range of subjects to offer. *It was agreed that an effort should be made to induce the approving Authorities to relax the conditions laid down for beginning the course.'*

The minutes of the following November meeting reveal that this request was turned down by the Authorities.[24]

Full-time advanced courses were not always easy to launch in the Management Department either. At a May 1964 meeting of the Management Advisory Committee, the Principal announced that the college's request to run a full-time Management Diploma course had been approved.[25] Some members of the Committee, however, expressed doubt about whether firms would be prepared to support such a course. It seems that for a long time they were correct in their suspicions, for it was not until as late as 1968 that the head of department was able to announce that this course was at last on a sound footing.[26]

Next to the Management Diploma course, the Department's most advanced full-time course was that leading to a Higher National Diploma in Business Studies. From an assessment of the numbers of students sitting their examinations for this qualification in June 1965, it seems reasonable to conclude that this course was running on a precarious basis, and this despite the fact that it had been established for a few years. The number of students sitting their first-year examination of this two-year course was only 13, and two of these students had repeated the year's work. Nine students took their final examination that year and one of these had repeated the final year of the course.[27]

Finally, with respect to full-time and sandwich advanced work, an issue that affected the Departments of Engineering, Science and Management alike was the refusal by the Regional Advisory Committee in 1965 to accept schemes submitted by the college for full-time and sandwich courses leading to degrees of the Council for National Academic Awards.

[24] Minutes of a Science Advisory Committee Meeting, 25 November 1964. From the Principal's Report to a meeting of the Committee in the same month the following year, it can be seen that an HND Sandwich course in Chemistry started with only 12 students and one in Applied Physics started with only 9 students. From verbal information given by members of staff it was learned that an HND course in Chemistry failed to start in the 1966–7 session for want of one student to make up a minimum enrolment figure of 10 insisted upon by the Department of Education.

[25] At the same meeting it was also announced by the Principal that the college had failed to get permission to run a full-time B.Sc. (Economics) course, a course that would have been administered by the General Studies Department.

[26] Announcement made at a departmental staff meeting.

[27] *cf.* Principal's Report to the Commerce Advisory Committee Meeting, 9 November (1965).

However, and this constitutes the second point, the college sometimes encountered just as much difficulty in developing part-time advanced work as full-time and sandwich advanced work.

At a December meeting of the Science Advisory Committee in 1961, for example, it was reported that numbers had not been adequate for the HNC course in applied physics to start in the previous September and the prospects for the following September were rated as 'not encouraging'. This prognostication happened to be a correct one for the Committee was told in the following November that the course had failed to commence that session for lack of the minimum number of students as required by the Ministry.[28] The competitive climate of inter-college relationships with respect to the part-time day work is also well illustrated by the following comment which accompanied the latter announcement:

> 'Unfortunately, some students who had prepared here for entry to the HNC course applied elsewhere.'

Dependence upon the activities of other colleges in the region is again illustrated by this statement made by one member of the Advisory Committee at its meeting the following May:

> 'Dr. Winkworth referred to the possibility of the . . . College giving up the HNC course in Metallurgy and wondered if approval for the course to be held in Jones could now be obtained.'[29]

Nevertheless, the Principal had to tell the Committee that the secretary of the Regional Advisory Council had written to say that it was unlikely that a proposal to run the course would receive support as existing courses in the Region were not full.

In the Engineering Department as early as November 1956, the problem of insufficient demand for an HNC course in Production Engineering was being faced.[30] The next year the Engineering Advisory Committee, discussing the department's proposal to offer thermodynamics as an

[28] cf. Principal's Report to the Science Advisory Committee Meeting, 4 November (1962).

[29] Minutes of a Science Advisory Committee Meeting, 8 May (1963). The Principal's Report to the Committee of 24 November (1965) shows that a post-HNC course in Modern Electronics (leading to L.Inst.P.) started with only 8 students and that, to quote from the report, 'Insufficient enrolments were received to justify the start of the new L.R.I.C. (Licentiateship of the Royal Institute of Chemistry) courses in Biochemistry and in Synthetic Organic Chemistry.'

[30] cf. Minutes of Engineering Advisory Committee Meeting, 20 November 1956. By the 1964–5 session the HNC course in Production Engineering was running but the examination results show that even by then only seven candidates could be mustered. (cf. Principal's Report to the Engineering Advisory Committee, 18 November, 1965.)

optional subject on the HNC course in Mechanical Engineering, had doubts about whether it would receive approval to buy the necessary equipment as two neighbouring colleges were already running the subject as an option.[31]

It is to the field of short courses that we turn for our final example of the college's pursuit of advanced work and the difficulty faced in so doing.[32] Until now we have relied mainly upon documentary evidence. On this occasion we shall use some of the verbal statements collected from members of staff in the course of our interviews with them. Firstly some examples of comments made by members of the Engineering Department about short courses.

A principal lecturer:

> 'I get a little worried about the number that are offered and are not running. I try to make sure it doesn't happen though, of course, it does sometimes.'

A senior lecturer:

> 'I did something on analogue computers but that wasn't well attended. Then I did one on lasers that was not well attended. Then I tried to do a residential course on automation for the small firm but it didn't run because of lack of support. You have to scour the country to get a course on.'

An assistant lecturer:

> 'There must be several courses that never reach the teaching state because there is no demand for them and no need . . . there were two that I was supposed to run but they didn't materialise – one student appeared for one.'

Secondly, a selection of those made by members of the Management Department.

A principal lecturer:

> 'We have concentrated too much on short courses – from the status viewpoint.'

[31] Minutes of an Engineering Advisory Committee Meeting, 20 November (1957.)
[32] Short courses were normally included in the 'advanced work' categories according to the Chief Clerk. See also the comments of Heads of Departments, page 39, concerning this point. The expansion of short courses may also be accounted for in other terms, namely their use as a promotion device (see Chapter 4). However, it is unlikely that they would have served this purpose had they not also been forms of 'advanced' work.

A senior lecturer:

> 'Occasionally there are some useful ones. But there is a limit – some are forced through, numbers are scrounged.'

A senior lecturer:

> 'We have to give up rooms or run shorter long courses because of these short courses. Then the latter may not run, or will run with very minimum numbers, whilst I have had to turn down students for courses.'[33]

A senior lecturer:

> 'I was told that they were a question of prestige, by the powers that be: "We know they won't run but they look good, they sound good." After a battle I managed to get them cut down in our section. In my experience most of them never get put on because there are no applicants.'

A lecturer:

> 'I don't think there is a real demand for such things. They're just there to create a handbook which looks very nice.'

A lecturer:

> 'In our section we run one-day courses and conferences. A good idea, but after a time you have to scrape around for topics and students.'

Conclusion

It was not possible to regard the changing structure of Jones College as simply the reflection of a changing pattern of demand. Had the strength of demand been the main criterion for the selection of students to fill the college's limited accommodation, then there seems little doubt that there would have been a greater concentration of effort upon the more junior work.

Of the relationship between Jones College's course of development and official policy two things are worth noting. Firstly, as we have pointed out, the 1944 Education Act said, in effect, that there should be co-operation between the various bodies responsible for the provision of further education facilities. On more than one occasion we have seen that the spirit in which Jones College conducted its relationships

[33] The students referred to by this lecturer are ones who would enter for the junior level secretarial courses.

with other institutions was one of competition.[34]

Secondly, despite their ambiguities, the essence of subsequent major official statements was that advanced work should be confined to the regional colleges unless demand was particularly strong elsewhere. Jones College, however, made persistent attempts to launch further advanced level courses even when the market stubbornly refused to show an interest.

In other words, forces at the local level seem to have played a considerable part in determining the nature of the college's ambitions and development. The relationship between the local education authority, the college governors and the staff is one that we have not been able to comprehend fully for lack of sufficient data. Given a permissive local authority and governing body, however, the power of the staff could be considerable. As can be ascertained to some extent from the conversations that have been reproduced in this chapter, heads of departments and staff were playing a positive part in course decision-making. Appendix III contains extracts from an interview obtained with a senior college administrator, a man who had been with it since almost the beginning. From this interview one gains the impression that the part played by the staff was a considerable one.

[34] It should perhaps be emphasised that we are not maintaining that the college was unique in its attitude. The following comments, made by members of staff during interviews, provide examples of the general climate of interaction among colleges in the region, and the region was probably no different from other parts of the country. A senior lecturer in the Engineering Department said:

'The fundamental problem is duplication of courses between colleges, Jones, . . . and . . . , each college has only 8 or 12 students on them. This is a colossal waste of lectures, three people preparing the same information, and an inefficient use of resources, such as laboratory equipment. The machine tool laboratory here here has £40 000 of equipment in it and similarly, so has . . . and . . . .'

Whilst a senior lecturer in the Science Department indicates how lack of official liaison between colleges in the region was circumvented by individual members of staff:

'I think the liaison with . . . is very poor. We have courses with four or five students on them and they have the same ones with four or five. For colleges to be competing with each other is ludicrous. Both . . . and us were doing ONC and there arose the question of who was to do the HNC. Jones got it going but . . . didn't mention to their students to come here for the HNC — they would say go anywhere but Jones. But we are now getting more students because one chap has gone from here to teach at . . . and another has come from there to teach here. Thus we are getting more students through these rather than official channels.'

4. The Staff of Jones College—Some Characteristics

Information about the methods used for obtaining data on the staff of Jones College is available both in the Introduction and in Appendix IV.

Background Experience and Teacher Training

Table 6 gives the working experience of the main staff sample prior to their appointment to Jones College.

Table 6. Full Time Work Experience

No previous experience		2
School teaching		12
Further Education teaching		15
Industry and Commerce		43
Local and Central Government		15
Forces		30
Miscellaneous		5
	TOTAL	122*
	N	57

*Some respondents had had more than one kind of previous work experience

Out of the fifty-seven respondents only nine had had either no previous experience or teaching experience only prior to joining the college. Of these nine people six were members of the General Studies Department.

Table 7. Teacher Training

2 years or more full time		3
1 year full-time or sandwich equivalent		16
1 year or more part-time		4
A short course*		7
No training (or less than above)		27
	TOTAL	57

* 1 month or over full-time; 2 months or over part-time

The department with the highest proportion of people having had one year or more of full-time training was the General Studies Department, where eight of the eleven respondents had received training. Of the twenty-seven respondents who had had no training at all, twenty had had no previous teaching experience before taking up their Jones College appointments.

47

Reasons for Entering Further Education

Respondents were asked to explain why they transferred from their last job – whether it was in a school, industry or elsewhere – to further education and, if they had not been employed previously, why technical college teaching was chosen.

Table 8. Reasons for Entering Further Education %

Intrinsic aspects	17
Economic and allied aspects	18
Disliked, or frustrated in, industry, etc.	12
Disliked, or frustrated in, school teaching	6
Wanted a change	10
Wanted a job enabling more time for other activities	6
Fortuitous, looking for any job	6 *
Miscellaneous	4
TOTAL	79†
N	57

* 3 people were looking for any 'teaching' job
† Some respondents gave more than one kind of reason

Table 8 represents an attempt to classify the answers to this open-ended question. Under 'intrinsic' aspects of the job have been included such reasons as wanting a job with more freedom, an opportunity to utilise knowledge possessed, a job with more interest, or the answers of those who said simply that they had enjoyed their previous part-time teaching experience. Answers classified as 'economic and allied' include those containing references to pay, the stability of the job, prospects and working conditions. In the case of those who replied in terms of needing a change or a new experience and those who were frustrated or disliked their previous jobs, it is possible to argue that they are using reasons of an 'intrinsic' nature. However, we felt that on the grounds of their neutral attitude towards teaching *per se*, such answers deserved a separate category. The kinds of 'other activities' for which some people thought that teaching would be convenient included business side-lines, research, religion and seeing more of the family.

Unsatisfactory though this kind of treatment is in many ways,[1] it is interesting that the 'teaching as a vocation' kind of attitude that one expects such a question to bring out appeared seldom here. In other words,

[1] It is difficult to decide the length to which the interviewer should go in pressing a respondent to answer a question: to decide when his initial response should be accepted and when he should be asked to develop this further.

there was very little about these answers to suggest that the college was staffed by individuals who had left industry or other jobs to teach in further education because of a strong sense of missionary zeal. The fact that so few had undergone full, if any, form of teacher training suggests a similar conclusion.

A few quotations from respondents' answers will be given in order to transmit more fully their character.

An Engineer:

> 'It was nothing more than because I was on the lookout for a profession which offered something better. If industry had offered something better I would have stayed.'

An Engineer:

> 'I had been with the firm for nine years and for the last couple of years I had done a couple of evening classes at Jones. This job came up and I thought it would save commuting to London. Also, promotion was very tardy in the firm and this job meant an immediate increase in pay and the loss of a couple of hours travelling. Even if I had got another job in industry it would still have meant travelling up at £15 per quarter for a season ticket.'

A Manager:

> 'There is no straight answer. The outfit I was with looked like packing up and there was an argument over policy. I knew I would have to leave if I was wrong and if I was right it would mean that the firm would fold up – either way I would have to go. Also I needed a change. I felt that I'd done all I could in industry. Thirdly, only this was the strongest reason, a relative became my responsibility and I knew that if I taught I would have the holidays and more time generally.'

A Manager:

> 'I found I liked teaching in the Department of Scientific and Industrial Research and the conditions of service in the Civil Service, but the pay and prospects caused me to look around for something else. I was on the top of my grade and for the next grade for promotion you needed to be 45. I thought one would have to work too hard in private consultancy – having to charge around the country – whereas in teaching there would be a more settled home life and time for private consultancy.'

49

The Technical College Teacher's Role

As has been pointed out, a technical college of the Jones College type is a complicated organisation and this means that there are a great many administrative and clerical tasks to be carried out. A feature of the management of such colleges is that a great deal of this work is in the hands of the teaching staff. Just how important a part of their job this element seemed to the Jones College staff themselves can be judged from the following responses to a question asking the fifty-seven members of the sample to estimate how much of their time spent in the college[2] went on teaching, lecture preparation and marking and how much of it went on administrative duties of one kind or another.

Table 9. College Time Spent on Administration

Amount of time %	Number
10% or less	14
11% – 20%	16
21% – 30%	11
31% – 40%	7
41% – 50%	4
Over 50%	5
	57

It is dubious whether these figures give an accurate picture of real work patterns and indeed respondents frequently said that they found such a calculation difficult to make. However, and this was the aim of the question, these answers do indicate how respondents felt these two components, teaching and allied tasks and administrative tasks, were balanced in their timetables. In interpreting these answers it must be remembered that heads of departments were not among the sample population.

We attempted to trace the feeling about this duality in the technical college teacher's role both by direct questions and by indirect methods, such as asking whether anything irritated them about their job. The kind of direct attack on the administrative duties that the following respondent made was not frequent:

[2] Members of staff were required to attend the college for ten sessions per week. A session could be either a morning, an afternoon or an evening and this amounted to a required period of attendance of 30 hours per week.

'I have one big groan and that's the idea of having to be a salesman as well as a teacher. The one thing I haven't liked doing is hawking courses around to get students . . . I feel that if they want salesmen types they want a separate branch of people.'

More often administration was attacked not for its existence but for its pettiness. The following outcry came from a man who had talked happily about initiating courses and conferences:

'What is a senior lecturer? I may have misjudged the job but it's surely not for marking-up registers. You don't pay a person my salary for this, this sort of thing is for clerical workers.'

Outright expressions of satisfaction about having a job with two sides to it was quite a common reaction.[3] Asked whether he would prefer to do all teaching or all administration, one respondent replied, for instance:

'Neither. I would prefer to do both. Anyone who does purely organising does get out of date, and anyone who does just teaching doesn't know the other side of things.'

Some, such as the following man, plumped for the job with more administration:

'I would prefer the administrative job but for the fact that I feel that the teaching wouldn't be done as I would like it on the course I was organising.'

This preference for the administrative side of the job came in its most extreme form from a respondent whose own position in the college had been altered by the creation of a new post:

'The bit of the job that interested me has been taken away, that is the organisation, the bit I thought that I was good at. Because I wouldn't call myself a good teacher.'

Thus there appeared to be no general feeling that the technical college teacher was having his professional status undermined by the inclusion of an administrative element in his job except where the duties involved were of an extremely elementary nature. This willingness to see the role as a wider one than just teaching would appear to be related to those factors identified earlier with this body of staff – the

[3] Indeed we found that a question asking respondents whether, if it came to the point of a choice having to be made, they would choose a job that was all administration (which would include course administration) or one that was just teaching, had to be abandoned because so many people felt unable to make such a choice.

non-teaching occupational background, the relative lack of teacher training, and the non-vocational attitude towards teaching as a career. We shall proceed to suggest that two other factors may be involved: the nature of the teaching function itself and the part played by research and publication in the life of Jones College.

Teaching

As Table 1 indicates, the bulk of the student enrolments was for short courses and part-time day or evenings-only courses, thus, and as was explained earlier,[4] much of the teaching in the college was on courses that were abbreviated or fractured by the standard of other parts of the educational system. This meant, moreover, that student-staff relationships were often transitory and the number of students dealt with by each member of staff was large. All this, it was thought, would be likely to have implications for the intrinsic satisfaction to be derived from the task of teaching.

Let us look first of all at some of the comments made by ex-school teachers. A middle-aged man who had spent all his working life in grammar schools apart from the three years he had been at Jones, said that he often felt that he would like to go back to a school but he believed that his age was against him. His opinion about teaching his subject at Jones was as follows:

> 'The part-time day courses are far from ideal. I get bored with them; it's cramming – more so than in a school . . . I enjoy the HND work but it is not as satisfying as the sixth form . . . A lot of what goes on in the College as a whole is bogus, a lot is not really worth the effort. The whole thing, the educational intent, is magnified beyond what it is . . . The students I take on the Chartered Accountancy and the ACCA part-time day courses I feel are here on false pretences: they get only 1·5 hours from me per fortnight which is ridiculous.'

A Language teacher who had previously taught in girls' grammar schools spoke similarly:

> 'I would like less classes and more time with those who looked as if they had a possibility of making some use of what I teach. I have to teach too many people whose courses pay lip service to languages and therefore give very little time per week to them and as a result you can't do much . . . As far as the work is concerned I would rather work in a good girls' grammar school.'

[4] *cf.* Introduction page 11.

52

Finally, a woman who had been at Jones for four years and whose other experience had been in secondary modern schools felt that in a school

'You see a lot more results of your work, especially in a subject like physical education. You have them for five years and you see things building up.'

The reason she left school-teaching was that she could not supervise Saturday matches after she had had children.
It was not only those with school-teaching experience who felt that there were shortcomings to teaching in further education. The following comment was made by a man who, before joining Jones, had been an accountant in industry:

'There is less personal times with the students than I should like. In the case of evening class students this is a sheer grind; I can't give them as much attention as is needed. On full-time courses I can do a little case-study work which involves a little more involvement but even there I can't seem to have enough time on this subject – in the case of the DMS course I have them for 22·5 hours in all and it is absolutely impossible to cover the course in this time.'

A Science teacher, whose previous occupational background had also been in industry, felt the fault of his job was that

'It is too much examination orientated . . . All the time you are aiming for an examination and consequently it's difficult to put over many of the basic principles and the background of science that I feel students should have. There is so little time, it's just flog, flog.'

Whilst the following teacher in the Management Department was overheard saying in the staff room one day.

'I'm so bored with constantly repeating the same old things. I find I do it so much I don't even believe it myself, I'm not listening to myself. The problem is that I'm doing all short courses . . . So every week you repeat the same thing. Even if one week it's a group of seamen the course is the same only the examples change.'

One index of the intensity of staff-student relationships is the extent to which staff invite students home. Out of the fifty-seven respondents, forty-three had never invited students to their homes, five had hardly ever done so, seven said they did so occasionally, and two thought they did so frequently. Interesting in themselves were the comments that accompanied the answers to this question. For instance, a General Studies Department lecturer said:

> 'I never really get to know them. Half you don't even know the names of because you don't see them often.'

Whilst one of the grammar school teachers whose statement we previously quoted from also said:

> 'Since I have been at Jones I never invite students home. At school I did so frequently. Some of the sixth form still come on holiday with us; I don't feel I know them well enough at Jones.'

Had the teaching task been more attractive, less hard work and more rewarding, it is not unlikely that there would have been less willingness to invest time in non-teaching activities.

Research and Publication

For the university teacher administrative duties compete for his time with not only teaching but also with research, a source of intrinsic satisfaction as well as a means of furthering a career. What was the place of research and publication in the life of Jones College?

Although only three of the Jones College sample possessed higher degrees there were only three other people registered on courses leading to Masters' degrees and one registered for a PhD, whilst two of these, one being the PhD student, admitted that they were not serious about the course. Discounting the three people already in possession of higher qualifications, whether or not a person was working for a higher degree was one way of assessing the amount of research activity going on among the staff, since it was unlikely that a person not already in possession of such a qualification would fail to use a piece of work for that purpose where possible. In fact all three of the scientists with higher degrees commented on their lack of activity in the field of research since they had been at Jones.

The problem about using registration as a criterion of research activity was that it failed to cover those people with insufficient academic qualifications to obtain university recognition to read for higher degrees. Yet to ask people merely if they were engaged in any 'research' was to invite answers of such variety that classification would have been out of the question. To cope with this problem, staff were asked about publications and this question revealed that four people were either currently engaged in writing books, or had written books since they had been in further education, one person had contributed a chapter to a book since he had been working at the college and another had participated in the writing of a pamphlet since he had been there.

Nevertheless, the overall impression gained was that research and publication were activities pursued by a very small minority of people in the college. However, the conditions in the college were not conducive to such activity. Technical College teachers have heavy teaching loads in comparison with university teachers.[5] A member of staff who embarked upon a piece of research or a course could, with the sponsorship of his head of department, submit an application to the local authority for a reduction in his teaching load. If this was successful normally an allowance of three hours would be made. However, for an assistant lecturer with a commitment of up to 24 contact hours a week, such a reduction was not a great deal. Whether the allowance was of any use at all depended upon the distribution of the rest of his teaching hours.

Even if it was unnecessary for the person to go outside the college in order to attend classes in connection with his course, use laboratories or libraries, or collect data, because of the college's overcrowded staffroom facilities and a library too small to take even all of the students wishing to work in it, somewhere away from the college was essential for work needing close concentration. The problem of finding a suitable place to do even lesson preparation is illustrated by the following comment made by an engineer:

> 'the opportunity for preparation is a big disappointment – if you have the time you are inconveniently placed. Three of us share a dusty

[5] Appendix III of the Robbins Report on Higher Education gives statistics on the teaching hours of university and further education staff and from these the following comparisons have been drawn up for the three grades, senior lecturer, lecturer, and assistant lecturer for the 1961–2 session. (Unfortunately these comparisons are not precise ones because of the way in which these statistics have been presented)

University Teachers	Weekly teaching hours of the largest percentage	%
Senior lecturers	5– 8	27
Lecturers	9– 12	28
Assistant lecturers	5– 8	34

Technical College Teachers (excluding CAT's)	Weekly average teaching hours
Senior lecturers	17·0
Lecturers	19·8
Assistant lecturers, Grade B	22·1

Committee on Higher Education, *Report on Higher Education,* Cmnd. 2154, Appendix 3, Table 69, page 69, and Table 21, page 122, London (1963).

old dark room and to get to it you have to go through a classroom. So I find that if I have six hours to spare, between morning and evening lectures, it is often wasted. I find my most effective work is done at home.'

But there was the problem of getting a suitably arranged timetable out of the complicated network of courses that take place in a technical college, as is illustrated by the following assistant lecturer:

'When I left university I thought it was more likely that one would be able to do research in a technical college than elsewhere. But it's clear now that if you are going to do research and your stint in the classroom and laboratories there will be no time to do anything else – I have no illusions about this. What's the good of three hours per week . . . But I am envisaging working for a further qualification, the problem is I need a laboratory. The only way round this is to attend a university on a part-time basis. The nearest place is London and I've worked it out that I need to go in for six hours. I am now wondering whether it is possible to get the classes organised so as to give me this free period.'

Perhaps even more revealing is the fact that a senior lecturer in the Science Department with a PhD and a number of years of post-doctoral research behind him, a man who would find operationalising a piece of research less difficult than most others, when asked about ways in which his job at Jones College had failed to match up to his ideal, said:

'It's mainly the way that research facilities haven't appeared . . . I would have like to have taken on more research – and I was given a promise about this at my interview – but neither the time nor the money has been forthcoming.'

Research, therefore, was not a viable source of job satisfaction for the Jones College teacher and thus it probably did not stand in the way of administration to any significant degree.

Conclusion

On the basis of the information given by those members of staff who were interviewed and the relatively low incidence of proper teacher training among them, it seems reasonable to conclude that the initial orientation towards the job by the staff of Jones College contained a strong instrumental element.[6]

[6] *cf.* A. Etzioni *A Comparative Analysis of Complex Organisations,* New York, (1961), pages 8–11 for a typology of involvement on the part of an organisations

Scope for the kinds of intrinsic job satisfaction normally associated with educational institutions was relatively limited at Jones College, the mechanics of the teaching situation being such that the act of teaching was more of a chore than it has to be in schools and universities and the opportunity for research being restricted. We are not arguing that the relationship between the demand for intrinsic and extrinsic forms of job satisfaction is necessarily of a compensatory nature. But to the extent that the need for the latter can be affected by the amount of intrinsic satisfaction to be derived from a job, it was not to be expected that the instrumental attitudes found to mark the process of job choice among the staff of Jones College would be radically diluted once they had had experience of the work itself. Indeed such attitudes may even have been strengthened. [7]

The fact that the respondents were in no way disposed to presenting their reasons for entering further education in a less instrumental light to the interviewer may indicate that little revision had taken place in their thinking, or, if it had, it had taken place in the reverse direction. That is to say, their initial expectations that the job would be a satisfying one had either been forgotten or, being unfulfilled, were deliberately not recalled.

It is true that administrative tasks appeared to afford a certain amount of satisfaction, but for most members of staff there was still a heavy load of contact hours to be worked through and it seems unlikely therefore that this was a factor that could have radically altered matters. Of course it is possible to obtain satisfaction from the general climate of an institution in which one works, irrespective of the tasks one is occupied in carrying out. The following two chapters deal with the climate of Jones College but a few words on the subject will be said here.

The climate of a college is the product of a complicated process involving what members of staff bring into the work situation and the context of their interaction with one another. The fact that the staff of Jones College were interested in the extrinsic aspects of their jobs such as pay and prospects would be of fundamental importance for the climate of the college. It was to be expected that there would be particular concern among them over college policies that affected their positions and prospects, and that conflict would occur where such policies affected

participants. Etzioni uses the categories alienative, calculative and moral involvement and in these terms the staff would appear to register a low for amoral and a high for calculative involvement. On all future occasions when these terms are used it should be assumed that they take Etzioni's meanings.

[7] *cf.* the Introduction for a discussion of the relevance to the technical college teacher of conflict between career orientation and commitment to students.

them differently. Furthermore, given a situation, like that of Jones College, which demonstrated the possibilities of individual advancement, the climate was likely to feel a competitive one in which to work.

It was found that administrative tasks, though quite an important feature of the work in the college, aroused surprisingly little resentment among the staff. This attitude towards administration is perhaps further support for the idea that among these teachers moral commitment, in Etzioni's terminology,[8] to teaching was not strong and, or, an indication of the limitations on the intrinsic satisfaction to be derived from teaching and research in the college.

[8] A. Etzioni, *A Comparative Analysis of Complex Organisations, op. cit.*

5. The Staff Climate of Activity

Table 10 gives the distribution of staff between different grades below the level of head of department for the 1965–6 session.

Table 10. Staff Grades

	Principal lecturer		Senior lecturer		Lecturer		Assistant B		Assistant A		Total	
	No.	%	No.	%	No.	%	No.	%	No.	%	No.	%
Engineering	2	4·4	10	22·2	6	13·3	0	60·0	0	0	45	100
Building	0	0	1	8·3	2	16·7	9	75·0	0	0	12	100
Science	1	3·8	8	30·8	9	34·6	8	30·8	0	0	26	100
Management	6	9·5	20	31·7	23	36·5	14	22·2	0	0	63	100
General Studies	0	0	2	5·7	7	20·0	25	74·4	1	2·9	35	100
Catering	0	0	1	3·1	5	15·6	26	81·3	0	0	32	100

Source: College General Office files.

From this it can be seen that the Management Department enjoyed a greater proportion of highly graded posts than the other departments. The distribution of graduate and non-graduate staff is given in Table 11.[1] From this it becomes clear that departments differed quite radically in terms of the educational backgrounds of their staff.

Table 11. Staff Qualifications*

Department	PhD	First or other degree	No degree
Engineering	0	6	40
Building	0	0	13
Science	6	18	3
Management	0	29	34
General Studies	0	21	15
Catering	0	3	33
Total	6	77	138

* Including Heads of departments.
Source: College Prospectus.

[1] The sample threw up quite well the range of qualifications, as we show below. (It must be remembered that the sample did not contain heads of departments, whereas these are included in Table 11.)

	Engineering	Building	Science	Management	General
Ph.D.	0	0	3	0	0
First degree	2	0	4	10	6
No degree	12	4	1	10	5

By comparing these two tables it is revealed also that the distribution of highly graded posts did not correspond to the distribution of graduates; the Management Department had proportionately less graduates than either the Science or the General Studies Departments yet it was slightly better endowed with senior posts than the former and considerably better endowed than the latter with such posts. Neither was it the case that the number of graduates in a department was always related to the level at which work was classified. Earlier, in Table 5, it emerged that the General Studies Department had the largest proportion of its work classified as low level work of all departments, yet here it can be seen that this department had proportionately more graduates than all the other departments except for the Science Department. Such structural features were part of the background to the staff climate.

Promotion

Table 12 gives the answers to an open-ended question on ways of 'getting on' in the college.[2] It was particularly noticeable that references to promotion as a reward for good or conscientious teaching were completely lacking. Indeed if the subject of teaching was raised in the context of answering this question it was done in order to point out the negative part it played in obtaining promotion, as, for instance, in the case of the following response to the question of how to get on in the college:

> 'Be a good actor, sell yourself. It's not a question of being a good teacher. It's the same in any job. Have the ear of the appropriate Principal Lecturer or Senior Lecturer and be efficient in your job, on the surface.'

Even a principal lecturer, a man who would play an important part in promotion, was doubtful about whether good teaching was always rewarded:

> 'I would like to say that the person who gets on is the person who teaches most effectively, but it doesn't happen in every case. Promotion slips by, others get on by being in the limelight.'

The second point that emerges from these answers is that little store was set by research and publication as a mode of ascent through the college. For instance, a scientist, who despite having a PhD was still placed only at lecturer grade, when asked what the effect of having published

---

[2] These categories are not discrete ones, of course; for example, 'Building up courses' and 'Administration' have much that is common about them.

Table 12. Avenues of Promotion

There is no internal promotion*	17
Luck, being on the spot at the start	11
Administration	12
Building up courses	16
Having a gimmick, a specialism	8
Selling yourself	9
Getting on with superiors, being orthodox	16
Knowing the Principal's weakness	2
Qualifications†	8
Publication and research	2
Miscellaneous	4
Don't know	2
	107‡
N	57

* Six of these respondents referred to methods that used to work and these have been included.
†Often this meant a degree.
‡Some respondents gave more than one method.

some papers whilst at Jones had been on his career, replied that it would have made no difference had he not published them:

'the hierarchy here are probably not aware of the fact'.

Thirdly, the answers frequently conveyed the feeling that there was a lack of confidence in the value of loyalty or hard work and integrity. As the table shows, a large proportion of the sample felt that internal promotion was unavailable.

'To get on you have to leave . . . If anyone asks for an increase in his grading in this department the Head is surprised by the person's temerity. There has been only one promotion in this department since I have been here,'[3]

[3] This point is reinforced by the answers to the question, 'From which direction do you expect your chances of career advancement to come, inside or outside Jones College?' These were as follows:

Inside	1
Possibly inside	3
Either or don't know	8
Probably outside	3
Outside	32
Neither	8
Miscellaneous	2
	57

said one respondent who was in his fourth year with the college. More to the point, however, were the accompanying suggestions that it was easier to get the better job if you were an outsider than an existing member of staff:

> 'One must look around for a post elsewhere. There is more chance here for the outsider. They prefer to bring in new blood – not necessarily younger but different people.'

Whilst such answers as the importance of luck, gimmicks, being able to sell oneself or ingratiate oneself with superiors and even references to the building up courses when this carried with it the implication that this was regardless of the needs of the college or community, all have the feel about them that it is qualities antithetical to hard work and integrity that are involved.

Turning to consider in more detail the factors that were regarded as instrumental in achieving promotion, it can be seen that high on the list of these was administration and its manifestations. An engineer who had been with the college for six years as an assistant lecturer told the following anecdote which illustrates not only the importance attached by him to administration in this context but also the unimportance of teaching.

> 'The way to get on is through administration. When I came to Jones it was a small place and one could watch what went on – I have seen people going up in this way. Take Bob Russell who is now . . . Bob Russell used to take my class for liberal studies and he would turn up for about one lesson in three and when he did he was late. Then in 1961, the year of the HMI's visit, he turned in an immaculate class record sheet, all filled in for the periods he wasn't there . . . As a consequence he was promoted because, they said, he was doing too much teaching as well as administration. No matter how good you are at teaching you never get the credit for it. It's only the things outside the classroom that count. Another fellow here is now a senior lecturer and he used to show up, give the class something to do and then disappear.'

As Table 12 indicates, course building was singled out in particular as a mode ascent. That this was essentially an administrative activity is clear when what was involved is described. Building up a course in the college would mean in practice either starting from scratch with an idea for a course, which would usually apply to short courses, or selecting a nationally recognised course that the college had not run before, then putting it up for approval to the Head of Department, the local authority or the Department of Education, depending upon the type of course it was.

A syllabus would have to be decided upon and sold to firms or the general public. Staff to teach on it and accommodation would have to be secured. A member of the Management Department, already a senior lecturer, described his own prospects as follows:

'the only way I'm going to get on is to develop Marketing and then I would be made a principal lecturer.'

The short course was frequently mentioned as useful in this context and the reason for this was partly that there were less restrictions placed by the authorities upon launching it.[4] Table 13 shows the answers to a question asking respondents about the extent to which they agreed with the suggestion that the incentive for running short courses was the possibility that promotion would lie at the end of doing so.[5]

Table 13. Motives for Running Short Courses

Agree the incentive is promotion	26
Partially agree	20
Disagree	7*
Used to be true	3
Don't know	1
Total	57

* 2 respondents said it was not true of
of their department but could be more so of
the college as a whole

Connected with course-building were those answers that referred to the usefulness of a gimmick or a specialism for getting on. For what was usually meant by these terms was an idea for a new course, preferably a new course that would be 'Jones on the map' as one person said, or the possession of something different in the way of skills or knowledge which the individual could capitalise upon by building up courses around it. An economist on the staff, for instance, lamented that his subject was the wrong one from the latter point of view:

'You have to find a highly specialised line and sell it. I don't think there is any future in economics. Everyone has done something of it and all have a go at teaching it, whereas marketing or work study are – at least they appear as if they are – highly specialised.'

[4] Courses of less than one month's duration full-time or 40 hours part-time did not have to be submitted for the formal approval of the Regional Advisory Council and the Department of Education and Science.

[5] It should perhaps be added that this was one of the few opinion questions that we 'closed' and it now seems to us that it was too loaded to be entirely satisfactory.

Perhaps the most surprising aspect of the other factors mentioned, the part played by luck, the need to sell oneself and be liked, etc., was that they were so much the same as those that one would expect to hear in replies to a similar question put to the employees of any business firm. To sum up, the reply of a man who had himself enjoyed a meteoric rise in the college, going from assistant lecturer on joining in 1962 at the age of 24 to senior lecturer by 1966, will be repeated. In order to get on, he said:

> 'One has got to accept administration and I think one must be acceptable to superiors, the Principal Lecturer and the Head of Department . . . There is an element of luck too, you have got to be in the right place at the right time.'

The 'Rat Race'

Many of the questions used in the previous section to convey respondents' opinions on the way the promotion system worked carried with them a note of censure. We turn now to an examination in more detail of the climate. It was noticeable that when members of the staff criticised the atmosphere in which they worked it was not so much the 'them' of a bureaucratic power structure who were admonished as the activities of colleagues.[6]
Colleagues were criticised for lack of dedication to the task of teaching. For instance, one entrant from the secretarial world was surprised to find that 'teachers weren't as idealistic' as she had expected them to be. Similarly an engineer was surprised that there was such a 'very small percentage of very dedicated people in the college'.
Colleagues were criticised for their careerism. Another engineer, asked whether anything irritated him about Jones College, replied:

> 'Careerism, particularly in the Engineering Department. People, instead of working with you, want to claim everything at your expense. One-upmanship. Equipment is ordered . . . without my being consulted and I'm the one who knows most about it. New courses are proposed in my field without consulting me.'

A scientist said that he did think 'there would be less of a rat race (in the college) than in industry, but if anything it was much worse'.

[6] *cf.* P. M. Blau and W. R. Scott, *op. cit.* paperback edition, Chapter 3, pages 62–63 (1966), for a comparison between bureaucratic and professional control structures, the former being based on a hierarchy of authority and the latter on the colleague group.

A lecturer on the point of leaving the Management Department to return to industry said:

> 'I suppose you could say I was naive about the political rat race in teaching. In industry there is a fairly clear cut division between management and men, and either you are working with the management or you are on the side of the unions. In this business you don't know who you are working for or which way they are working. The excuse is that everything is done for the students, but that's a very thin excuse. This personality struggle in teaching is difficult to cope with. You expect it in industry. In teaching there is no problem of the sack or being out of work yet there is this desire to score off one another.'

A lecturer who had recently been involved in a college dramatic production which, because of the expense involved, had become the centre of a controversy, felt that

> 'Everybody here seems to be too keen on pushing forward their image. Nobody wanted to know when it was thought that the production would be a flop; then they all wanted to climb on the 'bandwagon' when it turned out to be a success. Everyone is fighting for an empire and you have got to fight like mad to keep yours in one piece.'

Such comments were levelled at the general, overall climate. Others had to be seen against a background of cross-cutting sub-groups within the college. The main factors at the bases of these seemed to be the departmental structure and the educational and occupational backgrounds of the staff.

The Departments and Social Relationships

The departments were a feature of the college in a formal sense. Over the years, with the growth in size of the college, bureaucratic methods of administration had been adopted.[7] What was of interest was the extent to which this departmental structure penetrated the life of the college. Its part in determining the pattern of working relationships among the staff can be judged from their answers to a question asking them about the amount of contact they had with members of other departments in the course of carrying out college business. These answers are given in Table 14:

[7] cf. H. H. Gerth and C. Wright Mills (trans. and eds.), *From Max Weber: Essays in Sociology*, New York, pages 196–204 (1946).

Table 14. Contact Between Members of Different Departments over College Business

A great deal of contact	9
Some contact	19
Contact rare	24
No contact	5
Total	57

One point that emerged clearly was that the General Studies Department was the exception in the amount of working contact it had with other departments and this followed naturally from the fact that it was responsible for servicing the college as a whole for English and Liberal Studies – subjects which were included in some of the courses run by all of the other departments. Of the nine people who said that they had a great deal of contact with other departments, six were members of the General Studies Department and the other five members of that department interviewed all stated that they had 'some' contact. Once these are removed from the totals, inter-departmental contact tends to look rather thin.

It was felt that one factor contributing to the general atmosphere surrounding inter-departmental relationships would be the Heads of Departments. There are two ways in which they were potentially influential. They were recruiting into their departments people who were often without prior training for teaching or teaching experience, or further education teaching experience, thus it was possible that they would play some part in the shaping of the attitudes to the job acquired by these members of staff. Secondly, because of their positions of relative power within the college they could exercise some influence on its structure and thus on the working situation of the rest of the staff. To what extent did the Heads of Departments at Jones College regard themselves as partners in a joint educational venture and to what extent did they rule their departments as separate, even competing, empires? Some quotations from the comments of Heads of Departments used in Chapter 2 illustrate also the concern with their departments as individual entities and their preoccupation with building up the status of their particular departments. Perhaps this remark by another Head on the situation that faced him on taking over his department brings out even more the feeling of separateness between the departments:

> 'When I came there were only seven staff in the department and morale was very low. There had been no Head of Department between the February and the September and the department had been left to drift. Other departments started taking over rooms and secretarial staff; other departments were expanding and this one was standing still.'

Another way in which the same point shows itself is in the attacks, usually subtle, made by Heads on the conduct of affairs, or on the quality of the work, in other departments. For instance, one Head, talking about the difference between his department and others, said:

'We don't have to go out and get students: they come to us, unlike, say, the Management Department . . . All our courses are externally assessed and that's the way I like it. Every course is for an exam which is therefore an indication to the profession of our standard . . . I wouldn't like the system, say, in the Management Department where there is nothing at the end of a course to show what has been done. That's why, if you ask my men to put on a short course, they are very unenthusiastic. The thing is this: you put on a short course, hire a hotel, throw a lunch, etc., then at the end you say, "Well, that was a great success." But when you reflect on it what has been achieved?'

The same man was also sceptical about the statistics produced by the college on the distribution of advanced work between the departments:

'If I had a first year economics class in one of my courses, say, ONC, it is graded low. Yet when someone from the Management Department comes in to service it real problems occur. They are so used to teaching a superficial introduction to the subject on a short course (which is graded higher) that when they teach in this department the standard is inadequate, it isn't academic enough. I can honestly say that the only papers we have ever had back from the external assessors as below standard have been for courses that we have had serviced in this way.'

Another Head felt similarly about the way work was graded in the college:

'I feel that the academic work we do at Advanced level is the same as, or possibly more advanced than, that that is done in a short course in the Management Department. And if you take the statistics course in the Diploma in Management, for instance, then I feel that the level is lower than Advanced level GCE statistics. But because the Management Diploma requires candidates to have a degree or HNC then the course ranks as postgraduate, yet the academic content is relatively low level and bears no comparison to the usual meaning of the term postgraduate.'

The subject of the distribution of courses between departments was one which introduced an even stronger air of competition into matters. The General Studies Department was quite vulnerable to take-over bids. Past

67

policy had left it with an array of courses and some of these, on strictly rational grounds, were more in keeping with the activities of other departments. The Head of the department was quite content about this arrangement himself. However, other departments were not so pleased about the situation. The Head of the Building Department, for instance, would have liked to have had the gas fitting courses that were in the General Studies Department alongside courses in his department on plumbing. In the late nineteen sixties the General Studies Department did in fact lose a section – that devoted to trade union studies – to the Management Department and it can be seen that this was not parted with lightly by the Head of the General Studies Department's comment: 'but I managed to hang on to the Communications Unit'.

However, the General Studies Department was not the only department which had courses that interested other departments. The Head of the Building Department also expressed doubt about whether his department had received all the work it should have had when it was split from the Engineering Department; and he was particularly unhappy that so much of the construction industry's management level work was in the hands of the Management Department. In his turn, the Head of the Engineering Department was not sure that production management was the exclusive province of the Management Department.

An example of how the attitudes among heads of departments penetrated the work situation of members of their departments is the case of one member of staff who was concerned with management subjects in the courses run by his department. Asked if he called in people from the Management Department to service his courses, he replied:

> 'Not much because of the politics between our Head of Department and the Head of the Management Department . . . We have resources the Management Department needs and *vice-versa* . . .'

With regard to staff attitudes to the departmental structure, firstly, it was apparent that the distribution of courses was a subject which interested not only heads of departments but their staff as well. An excellent example of a field in which a number of interests clashed was that of Quality Control, the conflict occurring even between sub-sections of departments. According to a statistician in the Management Department, both his section and the production management section of the department, as well as members of the Engineering and Science departments, were interested in putting on courses in Quality Control. He told the following story:

> 'We put up courses in "Quality Control and Statistics for Science Students", but the Head of Department said that the Engineering and

Science Departments wouldn't like it. So we amended the title
to "Statistics for Scientists and Management". They have been
running the evening course in quality control but we have deliberately
avoided clashing with it. However, the production management
people insist that quality control is part of production management . . .
So now we have withdrawn from short courses on quality control.
Although the silly part about it is that we teach it on the full-time
courses, the HND, Diploma in Management Studies and the
Work Study courses. In the latter case that's part of the production
management section.'

(It was therefore a little disconcerting to hear a production manager
complaining still, during the course of an interview, about the way in
which the short courses on quality control run by his section were being
duplicated by the statisticians.) Then there is the case of a member of
the Building Department, on the point of leaving the college to
return to industry because his job had become repetitive, who declared
that he would not have had to take this step had his department been
able to retain courses lost to the Management Department on management
in the construction industry.

Secondly, staff were given to making comparisons between the state of
their department and that of others or to comparing their positions with
those of members of other departments. In this kind of activity the
Management Department tended to be singled out as a standard of
comparison. Sometimes it was the quality of the work that was looked
at, as in the case of this Engineer:

'They don't seem to have any standards. Where we have thrown
out people as not good enough for our department they take them
in and say what good students they are.'

Sometimes it was size. For instance, a lecturer in the Building Department
felt that there was:

'a tendency for oversize in the Business and Management Studies
Department which seems to overawe the remaining departments'.

A member of the General Studies Department considers both factors
in the following:

'One always like to see one's own department flourishing more . . .
I have the feeling that Management has grown a lot and is
outstripping what it should be doing – there's a lot of pomp and
façade there . . . Each department should be big enough and similar
enough to have self respect, at the moment the General Studies

Department falls short here . . . I think that eventually the General Studies Department will close up.'

Elsewhere it was comparisons with the gradings of Management Department staff that were made, although this was usually the issue at the bottom of comments like those above on size and quality of work.[8] For instance, a scientist, well qualified himself, said heatedly:

'What makes one so livid is to see people coming straight into the Management Department as lecturers. On one occasion the person had only just got his HNC in the department, whereas someone was taken on in this department at the same time as a Grade B who had a PhD and had done two years' post-doctoral research.'

Whilst a member of the General Studies Department put forward the case of himself:

'I think I am worth more than I get . . . In the Management Department high positions are held by people who have chosen teaching as a second choice whereas in General Studies we have chosen teaching first. It is almost a disadvantage to have gone to university: it is better to go into industry and then to come in as a senior lecturer. Dedicated teachers don't get the rates: those that come in through the back door get higher positions.'

Thus the departments constituted not only an official, or formal, feature of the college structure but also one real way in which, to some considerable degree, staff orientated themselves. This could perhaps be no better illustrated than by the role problems facing the liberal studies teacher in the college. As stated earlier, the General Studies Department was responsible for servicing the whole college for English and Liberal Studies. The organiser of these subjects for the General Studies Department saw the situation as one in which the liberal studies teacher struggled for autonomy against the desire on the part of the departments for complete authority over their students. He said:

'As a service department other departments say what they want us to do and when. It means they dictate, and that is bad. Take the . . .

---

[8] For example, the Builder who had said earlier that there was 'a tendency for oversize in the Business and Management Studies Department which seems to overawe the remaining departments', when asked whether he felt that this had any repercussions, replied:
'There are possibly quite a lot in terms of promotion throughout the college.'

Department, for instance. I was organising liberal studies for the whole college and yet the . . . Department said there *would be* a liberal studies examination the next week. I would like to have said that it depended upon us. There have been cases where students have told *us* that they are having a liberal studies examination the following week. This is the case of other departments dictating.'

A final comment on the penetration of the formal departmental structure into staff relationships is the pattern of staff association outside the college. Members of the sample were asked about the extent to which they visited colleagues in their homes and if such visiting that took place was exclusively among people drawn from within their own departments or not. These answers are given in Table 15, and from them it can be seen that such visiting as took place between members of the staff was more often among members of the same department than on a cross-departmental basis.[9]

Table 15. Visiting Among the Staff

	All visiting	Visiting across Departments
Does not take place	8	—
Rarely takes place	13	4
Occasionally takes place	29	9
Frequently takes place	7	6
	57	19

Educational Qualifications and Industrial Experience

As was noted earlier, the Jones College staff were characterised by a lack of uniformity in their educational qualifications. Was this something that was left behind on joining the college? Did the act of being asked

[9] The department which contained the largest number of staff with a tendency to visit across departments on more than 'rare' occasions was the General Studies Department. Of the nine people who said that they 'occasionally' made or received visits and that this could concern people from other departments, four were from the General Studies Department (the Engineering Department came next in this respect but it contained only two such people and the department was considerably larger). It produced also two of the six people who said that such visits 'frequently' took place.

71

to join the staff become a kind of ritual cleansing from which all emerged on an equal footing? It seems not.

Many of the non-graduates interviewed revealed themselves to be very conscious that they were non-graduates. Even a Head of Department said that he was very aware of the fact that his qualification was degree *equivalent*. Particularly strong feelings on the subject emerged among the members of one department. A man who was to leave at the end of the term said about his Head of Department:

'He is degree bonkers . . . A good example is Mr. Manners, a man who is extremely good at his subject and has been teaching at practically the highest level done in this college. Yet the Head wouldn't promote him – he didn't finish his degree for some reason – so Manners went out and got a job even over the head of another applicant with an MSc.'

His colleague reiterated this theme:

'Mr. James thinks everybody who isn't a graduate is useless. Since we have no graduates on the . . . side you have practically the whole section looking in the Times Educational Supplement.'

Possibly the point was put most succinctly by the member of staff who said,

'If I had my time again I would get a degree in anything.'

Another way in which the non-graduate's consciousness of not being in possession of a degree was revealed was in his use of graduates as a group of people with whom to find fault. The following is the above-mentioned Mr. Manners talking:

'Though I may be biased about graduates, they may have the ability but they are not good teachers generally. They have a "take it or leave it" kind of attitude which is all right for the more mature kind of students where they get on with the job, but it wouldn't work in a technical college because I don't think the students would be prepared to follow up the lecture. They need teaching.'

For this shorthand and typing teacher, having a non-graduate status made her so uncomfortable that she absented herself from the staff common room:

'I always thought that university people would be wider people than I find they actually are. Generally, if you teach shorthand and

72

typing you are looked down upon. I have heard men say, "If you do that you will be dropped down to shorthand and typing" . . . . . . You[10] are more acceptable in the common room by virtue of your subject and training than we are . . . People ask you what you do and when you reply they say, "Shorthand and typing – Oh!" Yet we have worked just as hard for our qualifications.'

The reverse process – of graduates distinguishing themselves from non-graduates – was also observable. This was particularly so among members of the Management Department. Here there were senior and principal lectureships in the hands of non-graduates and graduates were to be found in positions at the bottom of the hierarchy. Thus, this kind of comment,

'One thing that did shock me was to find at the level of Principal Lecturer someone without any academic or formal qualification,'

here made by a psychologist, was heard a number of times. An English graduate in the General Studies Department was not in sympathy with the college's efforts to launch CNAA degrees and he explained this in terms of the quality of the staff. Asked where he stood in the matter, he replied:

'On the side-lines roaring with laughter. Seriously though, the idea that a place like this should give degrees doesn't bear thinking about. It's ridiculous. When you look at the staff responsible for one part of the CNAA . . . less than half of them have degrees themselves.'

In addition, remarks were thrown out about the low intellectual standard among the staff, the lack of awareness in the college of how full-time further education should be conducted or ignorance of the academic standard of a degree. Such remarks revealed that the university graduates regarded themselves as different from, or superior to, the other members of staff even though they did not openly express such feelings to the interviewer. One such comment is the following, made by a lecturer in the General Studies Department:

'I don't think, at Jones, that there is much ability. Apart from a few exceptions I haven't felt that the intellectual calibre of the staff comes up to a Grammar School.'

Another example is provided in this French teacher's answer to a question which asked her whether she approved of the college running degree

[10] That is, the interviewer.

73

courses. Having said that in some ways she thought it was a good idea, she went on to say: 'But the staff as it at present stands hasn't a clue about the standard required.'

Just as educational qualifications were used as a criterion by staff for distinguishing between themselves, so was occupational experience. For instance, an engineer said:

'I came to develop the labs. They were in a disgusting state when I came. No thought had been put into them – my predecessor had no industrial background, he just taught from books. In this field you can't teach without industrial experience – this applies to all the courses: you can teach the theory from books but not the applied side.'

A Science Department graduate with industrial experience indicates in a more subtle way that the issue was there in the college:

'When I came in they said, "Has he got the industrial experience?", and I wondered why it mattered. Now I see the value of it. I can draw on it in my class: I can talk the same language.'

Whilst a lecturer in trade union studies, a member of the General Studies Department, felt that there was 'too much of the school-teacher about the college' and that his courses would give it 'more contact with industry, a more cosmopolitan, a more adult atmosphere' which would 'stir up the old English teachers.'

For their part, however, ex-school teachers were concerned about the harm the industrial influences were doing to the college. It was, in fact, an English teacher who said the following about the college:

'I don't think it attracts dedicated or professional teachers. It can't really because it's so diverse, so attached to industry. Subjects such as management and so on mean that people are not teachers in the educational sense, therefore it's not the place for one.'

Another ex-school teacher commented on a remark made by a principal lecturer about their previous Head of Department as follows:

'Plummer said, "Dickens is the best *boss* I have ever worked for". I didn't think of him as a *boss* but as a colleague.'

and in a few words revealed so much about the gap that he felt existed between himself and the industrially experienced Plummer.

So far the two sets of sub-groups – graduates and non-graduates, industrially experienced and non-industrially experienced – have been

74

treated for analytical purposes as discrete entities. In practice they
overlapped. Most of the non-industrially experienced were graduates
and most of the non-graduates were industrially experienced. However,
one set did not exactly superimpose itself upon the other as many of the
graduates were also industrially experienced and there were a few
non-graduate ex-school teachers on the staff. One effect of this
overlapping was that a confusion of educational qualifications and
occupational experience existed in the minds of some of the staff. This
can be seen clearly in the remark about promotion made by a General
Studies Department graduate reproduced on page 70, which contains
the assumption that the person who goes into industry will not have been
to university. In the following case a non-graduate equates being a
graduate with being remote from the real world of management:

> 'People in technical colleges who are promoted *must* have had
> management experience . . . For my part I don't have the right
> labels; I haven't a degree. But I think this is wrong thinking because
> everyday management doesn't use abstruse methods taught by
> graduates.'

Similarly, this sub-group structure overlapped with that created by the
departments. As Table 11 indicated, certain departments were staffed
almost entirely by non-graduates, for example, the Engineering and
Building Departments, whilst the Science Department was staffed almost
entirely by graduates. And generalising from our sample, in which –
of the fourteen respondents without industrial experience – eight were
members of the General Studies Department (and eleven members of
that department were interviewed in all), the General Studies
Department would appear to have the nucleus of the non-industrially
experienced staff.

Conclusion

A number of Jones College staff expressed the view – and such comments
were unsolicited by the interviewer – that the atmosphere in which they
worked was a competitive one. In addition to these direct comments, it
was observable from the attitudes and behaviour found among the staff
more generally that there was a tendency to regard other members of
staff as rivals. Without having suitable comparative material it is difficult
to judge whether Jones College was any different from other educational
institutions in this respect, although those people who had taught in
schools previously did comment on the lack of a community spirit in

Jones College compared with their schools.[11] There is ground for thinking that the technical college was likely to have a more competitive atmosphere than many other kinds of educational institution, and this is a reference to the part played by administration in its life.

Teaching and research are essentially private activities,[12] they take place largely unseen by other members of the staff and need not involve or have an impact on them of any kind. One consequence of this is that members of staff are not inconvenienced by such activities on the part of colleagues and thus no resentment is aroused. Another is that by their invisibleness these activities carry with them a certain amount of mystique. Thus the practitioner can be credited with special skills which deserve to be rewarded.[13]

Secondly, teaching and research are activities which, in most educational institutions, are open to all members of staff to pursue. This means that when one member of staff teaches or takes on research, his colleagues are not precluded from these activities as a consequence.[14]

Thirdly, they are activities that have about them what could be called a noble image. They are activities that society[15] regards on the whole as useful. Because of this, rewards for undertaking them are felt to be just. This image carries with it, too, the feeling that the person who undertakes

[11] For example:

'In the school there was more consultation between the staff, at lunchtimes we would see each other and could discuss matters. Here timetables don't coincide. 'At the . . . School we were only a 30 strong staff and we used to go around as a group . . . you have a willingness to help, to stay on after hours. Everyone here seems to be too keen on pushing their image forward.'
'There is more contact (between staff) in a Grammar School, you are thrown together much more. There was a closer affinity between the Latin, English and Music masters there than there is between the woodwork master and me here . . . Socially I do most things. The majority of people in my room don't attend things, I'm usually the only one. There is not enough social life here, no community spirit. Having been in a Grammar School I notice the difference.'
'I was not particularly interested (in the College's Staff Association Christmas and Summer dances). I would have gone to the school one but there seems no community at Jones and I didn't want to create one.'

[12] This description of teaching and research must be taken only as a comparison with the character of administration.

[13] cf. V. A. Thompson, 'Hierarchy, Specialization and Organizational Conflict', Administrative Science Quarterly, 5, page 493, for a discussion of similar imputations of superior ability to the holder of high office in a hierarchy because of the mystery surrounding what he actually does.

[14] Although, of course, it can happen that someone is unable to do the kind of teaching he wishes to do because the work has been acquired by a colleague.

[15] Members of staff are assumed to share these images.

such work is inspired not merely by calculative motives but also by a spirit of altruism.[16]

Finally, we tend to believe that the person who engages in such activities derives from them some degree of intrinsic satisfaction. This again leads on to the conclusion that the nature of that person's involvement is more than just calculative.

By contrast, administrative activities have much that is public about them: a good deal of what takes place under that title – at least in the Jones College context – does so under the gaze of other members of the staff. One reason for this at Jones College was that below the grade of principal lecturer, members of staff worked in communal rooms. Another, and this almost by definition, was that such activities would usually require the active participation of colleagues or have some kind of implication for them. It was quite likely, therefore, that some members of staff would be put to inconvenience by the administrative work of others – a new course might mean a different timetable or a shift of rooms. Moreover, because of the high degree of visibility of such work it can carry very little mystique. Observing what is entailed, other members of staff are likely to feel that they too could do the job and thus there is no feeling that rare skills are involved which deserve to be especially rewarded.[17]

Secondly, in the case of administrative tasks it is impossible for every member of the institution to become involved in work of the same quality. Only a limited number of people are needed for arranging timetables, rooms and syllabuses, and there are restrictions on the number of new courses that can be initiated. Thus, when one member of staff acquires such work he has precluded others from doing so.

Thirdly, there is very little of the noble image about administration. It is an activity that is regarded as useful only insofar as it paves the way for the really worthwhile activity to take place – teaching. And at worst it is

[16] Hence, according to B. Wilson, the conflict of the teacher between commitment to teaching and career orientation. (*cf. The Teacher's Role, op. cit.*)

[17] Indeed an attitude encountered among Jones College members of staff was that their superiors were particularly lacking in such skills. For example:

'I think it is disgusting that a man who is earning over £3000 doesn't do any teaching in the department. And what is more he is a terrible administrator. He is just sitting back and letting things slide.'

'(On entering further education) I was surprised by the lack of personnel ability of the people who are supposed to be in charge of the various sections . . . I haven't found one who is an able administrator.'

' . . . those in administrative positions are academics themselves and therefore are ill-fitted for it'.

thought of as parasitical.[18] Thus there can be a grudging attitude towards rewards for such work and little room for attributing motives of altruism to the person who engages in it. Finally, neither is it common to regard administration as an activity that affords intrinsic satisfaction to the performer and here again his motives for participation take on a particularly calculative appearance.

Insofar as this comparison is valid, an educational institution in which administration plays a large part, and particularly one in which this, rather than teaching or research, is regarded as the main criterion for promotion, is likely to feel especially career orientated and competitive as a place in which to work.

This is not to suggest that in administration at Jones College lay the entire explanation for the climate of the college. An interest in promotion had to be present for the means of attaining promotion to be important. In other words, it is suggested that the emphasis on administration was a factor that exacerbated rather than created a competitive climate.

As we have seen, there was a strong calculative element in the reasons given by members of the college for entering further education and we have suggested that it was unlikely that this disappeared after they had had some experience of teaching in the college. Calculative involvement is not, of course, synonymous with the desire for promotion. Indeed, some members of staff had said that they wanted a job which gave them more time for private activities, whilst others wanted to become teachers because of the security that this would bring, which did not mean that they wanted the bother of improving themselves. However, it does seem reasonable to assume that involvement of this kind would be on the whole conducive to the desire for promotion and, indeed, 'prospects' was a factor cited by some respondents as the motive for taking on the job. Moreover, the tone of the comments reproduced in this chapter bear out this assumption.

The other point raised in this chapter was sub-group identification. It did seem possible to trace patterns of such affiliations among the Jones College staff. The task of establishing the part these played in the life of the college was more difficult however. For example, it was hard to say exactly what their relationship was to its competitive tone: in some ways they appeared to be a casual factor, in others a product. In attempting to explain their origins, one has to look both to general social forces and to the college situation itself. From the very character of the groups it is clear that general social forces were important. However, the college must have presented a situation which was conducive for

[18] *cf.* Our daily references to 'Parkinson's Law'.

these forces to manifest themselves within it. A hypothetical situation can be constructed in which an organisation possessed such a powerful means of socialisation that a complete uniformity of attitudes and behaviour was achieved among its members despite their initial differences.[19] However, the task that Jones College had assumed was that of preparing a wide variety of students for an equally wide variety of roles in the outside world, and because of this what it required of staff was their familiarity with these diverse roles. Thus in one respect it could be said that the task of the college administration was to see that differences existed rather than to set about removing them. Certainly, as we have pointed out, there was little conscious attempt to do so through the means of insisting on teacher training.

Even though it was inherent in the nature of the work undertaken by the college that its structure would strongly reflect many outside social divisions, the significance of the differences between staff could be either heightened or reduced, albeit unintentionally, by the particular methods used to manage its affairs. The departmental structure was important in this respect. Most obviously this helped to perpetuate and extend the distinctions between artist, scientist, technologist and businessman. One of its more unintended consequences was that of separating, to some extent, the graduates from the non-graduates and, although to a lesser degree, the industrially experienced from the inexperienced. This physical separation determined not only formal work relationships between members of staff but also their friendship patterns, thus the latter network of relationships probably reinforced the formal structure.

Returning to the question of the relationship of group identities to the climate of the college, one point that deserves attention is the actual activity around which much of the rivalry among members of staff appeared to take place, namely, the initiation and management of courses. For such activity involved not merely particular individuals but groups of staff. For example, a number of graduates would take an interest in a proposed new degree course because they would teach on it. Other graduates in the college, people not directly involved in that particular course, might also be interested because by setting the right tone such work paved the way for later degree courses which would directly concern them. At the same time, the college's craft teachers, observing the steadily

[19] cf. E. Goffman, 'On the Characteristics of Total Institutions', *Asylums,* New York (1961), for a description of such a process. Uniformity of this kind could be achieved also as the result of selective recruiting on the part of the organisation or by self-selection on the part of the applicants. (cf. P. Selznick, *Leadership in Administration,* New York and Illinois (1957), for selective recruiting.)

increasing pressure on the college's facilities and sensing the complaints of their more educated colleagues that the college was being held back by its association with low level work, would view such proposals with apprehension. Seen in this way the college climate becomes the product of the play of group interests and conflicts.

Paradoxical though the idea may first seem, it is possible to regard the climate of activity as itself important for the staff structure. If as we have suggested career advancement was of particular interest to members of the Jones College staff, then it would be likely for individuals to compare their promotion chances with those of their colleagues. This process, we suggest, was one that would produce heightened sensibilities to the differences between them.

Moreover, it was to be expected that in a system where mobility was an accepted norm of behaviour, personal failure would be accounted for in terms of these group differences.[20] Finally, where a number of like-situated people are feeling injured, it would seem that the circumstances are right for a sense of solidarity to develop among them. For all these reasons, the college climate could be regarded not merely as a product of the staff structure but also as an influence in its turn.

[20] Some of the comments reproduced in this chapter illustrate such a process.

6. The Staff and the College Goals

As we pointed out earlier,[1] more than one department in the college had submitted proposals for degree courses at various times. The most recent occasion was the application made by the college to the Council for Academic Awards in 1965, when a number of degree courses were proposed. It has already been mentioned also[2] that for a number of years the subject of building an additional college in the locality, to take over Jones College's low level work, had been in the air. In April 1964, for example, the local press reported the Principal as having said that

> 'the college would eventually be split and the younger students in the main transferred . . . to a new junior section'.

We attempted to examine the attitudes of the staff towards these two fundamental issues.

Degree Work

Table 16 gives the answer to an open-ended question which asked respondents whether they thought that the college ought to aim at providing full-time and sandwich-based degree courses:

Table 16. Attitudes to Degree Courses

In agreement	15
In agreement, with certain reservations	8
Ambivalent attitudes	2
Not in agreement with certain modifications	1
Not in agreement	26
No opinion	4
Total	56*

* Question overlooked in the case of one respondent.

These responses were analysed on a departmental basis and this revealed that only one person from among the members of the Engineering Department interviewed was 'In agreement' with the policy, whilst the rest were all completely against it. (The one person who reacted favourably was a graduate.) Neither did anyone from the Building Department express a favourable reaction, although two people had 'No opinion' on the subject. In each of the three other departments used for the sample,

[1] *cf.* Chapter 3
[2] *Ibid.*

namely those of Science, General Studies and Management, the responses on this issue were mixed, although the balance of opinion was just slightly favourable to the policy in each case.

Thus it was the departments with non-graduate staffs that displayed the least amount of enthusiasm towards the idea of the college embarking upon degree work. However, it was not simply a case of graduates being in favour of degree work and non-graduates being against it, as Table 17 indicates:

Table 17. Attitudes to Degree Work by Educational Qualifications of the Staff

	Non-graduates	Graduates
In agreement	11	12
Ambivalent	0	2
Not in agreement	18	9
No opinion	3	1
Total	32	24

In other words, within the Departments of General Studies, Science and Management there were to be found non-graduates who liked the idea and graduates who objected to it.

It was not written into the interviewing schedule that a respondent must justify his answer to this question (for reasons which will be made plain in a moment); however, a certain amount of information of this kind was acquired. The arguments used by opponents of the policy tended to fall into two categories — economic arguments and educational arguments. Both graduates and non-graduates used those of the first kind, whereas those of the second tended to be produced by graduates.

The economic reasons given by opponents of the policy centred on the waste of resources involved in implementing such courses at Jones College when places were still vacant at other institutions or could easily be increased in them. A graduate member of the Management Department, for example, said of the policy:

'I don't think it's necessary because of the availability of other centres nearby.'

A principal lecturer in the Engineering Department, a non-graduate, having said he disagreed with the idea, continued:

82

> 'I think Pilkington and Prentice smacks of a good deal of commonsense – there are too many colleges with far too few students.'[3]

Educational reasons included the lack of proper facilities for students in a college like Jones College, inadequately qualified staff and the generally unsuitable educational atmosphere in the college for advanced work. These points are summarised in the following answer:

> 'It (the college) hasn't got the facilities, the atmosphere or the staff.'[4]

A colleague was rather more specific:

> 'On the basis of past experience I think it would be a bad thing to do high level work. I think there is a wrong attitude – a most casual approach. The concern has been solely a question of status. In the case of the B.Sc.(Econ.) somebody had an idea, it goes into the prospectus, and there is no thought about who is to staff it. In the case of CNAA it was "let's get a syllabus off this afternoon" sort of attitude.'[5]

A member of the Science Department felt not only that his department was too small to offer adequate facilities but also that it was doubtful whether the calibre of the staff was sufficiently high:

> 'The degree awarding places have attracted the best staff.'

His department, it should be remembered, had the most highly qualified staff in the college.
Conversely, it was the existence of suitably qualified staff that others used as reasons for supporting the policy. The following respondent is referring to the accountancy section in the following remark:

> 'Speaking for my own section, I think we should and are capable of doing this, we have the experience and the qualifications to do this.'

A scientist felt that the Science and Management Departments were, 'more than capable' and, when asked why he felt that the Management Department was capable, he replied:

[3] For the Pilkington and Prentice Reports see Chapter 2
[4] A lecturer in English, Department of General Studies.
[5] An assistant lecturer in English and Liberal Studies, Department of General Studies.

'Because it has some keen people. It doesn't lack keenness and with so many in the department there must be a statistical possibility that some are capable.'

Such comments are interesting for the additional material they provide on the college's climate of interaction, but whether they tell us a great deal about the determination of attitudes to high level work in the college is uncertain. It was for this reason that no systematic attempt was made to collect such explanations from respondents. It is impossible to calculate the extent to which a respondent's opinion on advanced work was the product of this kind of reasoning and to what extent it merely justified an opinion that had been formulated on other, personal or quite vague, grounds. The fact that attitudes for and against the degree work policy were not found to be randomly distributed among the departments, but to some extent clustered, suggests that one has to go beyond the interview to understand the situation more fully; in other words, that the general social setting needs examining.

Within the Engineering Department feelings against the policy ran particularly high. Take, for example, the following respondent's reply to the question of whether the college ought to aim at providing degree courses:

'On the engineering side, *no.* It's quite ridiculous on the engineering side . . . Why should we try and offer the same thing as people five miles away? "Jones College of Technicians", we should put up the sign at the front door and get on with it.'

To understand these feelings the following factors have to be borne in mind: the Engineering Department was staffed for the greatest part by non-graduates, and 50 per cent of the courses on which they taught were classified as 'lower advanced' or 'school level' standard;[6] it had been passing on low level work to other colleges;[7] and in 1965 a new Head of Department was appointed.

Because most of the staff of the Engineering Department possessed educational qualifications of below degree level[8] and had no teaching experience at advanced levels, direct involvement in degree work, should it be obtained, could have been anticipated by only a few members of of the department. On this basis not a great deal of enthusiasm towards the policy was to be expected among the engineers. However, they also

[6] *cf.* Chapter 3, Table 5.
[7] *cf.* Chapter 3.
[8] These were mostly Higher National Certificates and City and Guilds Full Technological Certificates.

had to watch the lower level work being rejected in order to make way for degree work. This could not have endeared it to them either, for there were presumably several people who would have endorsed one welder's remark that

> 'if the college is going to develop at the lower end then my chances of promotion are greater'.

In addition, the part played by the advent of a new head of department in the development of attitudes towards the policy deserves consideration. He had been an external candidate for the job and had taken it over from a man some twenty years his senior, a man who had retired after having been with the college since its early days.

So the new head was younger, but over and above this he seems to have projected an image of himself as a man of energy. These are not the characteristics of someone who is going to be regarded as likely to preserve the status quo and therefore the resentment towards him found among his staff at this time was predictable.[9] It may be, therefore, that the lack of enthusiasm for the degree work proposal among the engineers was in part a spillover effect: a reaction against a new man's policy. (By virtue of the fact that his department was fostering such proposals, the head would appear to his staff to be lending them his support.) However, there was another factor in the situation. The head of this largely non-graduate department was himself a graduate.

The Building Department was not involved in the process of submitting proposals for degree courses thus, for its members, even more than for the engineers, there was little prospect of deriving direct benefit from the policy. Therefore, it was not to be expected that they, either, would express a great deal of enthusiasm about it. That there was indeed a feeling of remoteness from the matter on the part of the builders can be ascertained from the use of the terms 'they' and 'us' in the following response given by a builder to the question of whether the policy was a good idea or not:

[9] Selznick has suggested that there will be hostility to change in an organisation where the process of 'value-infusion' has taken place; that is, when 'individuals become attached to an organisation or a way of doing things as persons rather than as technicians', when the organisation has become a source of personal satisfaction in its own right. (*Leadership in Administration, op. cit.* Chapter 1, page 17.) There is resistance to change in these circumstances, he says, because 'people feel a sense of personal loss; the "identity" of the group or community seems somehow to be violated' (page 19). It may be that the hostility to change found in Jones College can be explained in these terms in part, but the vital point would seem to be the nature of the change confronting the members of an organisation. The strength of such attachments is unlikely to be the same, or produce the same amount of resistance, where changes are seen as beneficial as where they are unattractive for those concerned.

C.A.C.I.A.T.C.—D
85

'It doesn't really matter to me. If they are going to do that kind of work it means that the likes of us must go.'

Although seemingly feeling remote from it, this did not mean that the builders felt untouched by the issue – a point which the above quotation illustrates also. The Head of Department had said[10] that, should such proposals receive the seal of approval, his department would have to move out of the college altogether because of the low level of its work and the pressure on accommodation that the new courses would create. It is not known whether this opinion had been broadcast to the staff but, as can be seen from the builder's comment above, such conclusions were not confined to the head of department. Thus, if they objected to the idea of moving, and some did as the following section shows, such a policy was not likely to please the building staff. Nevertheless, in contrast with the engineers, the reactions of the builders had an air of calm about them. For instance, of the four people in the sample who said that they had 'no opinion' on the subject of the degree work policy, two were builders. It may be that being confronted with an externally propelled force they felt in a particularly powerless position with regard to the future of the college, and this led to the adoption of a fatalistic attitude on the matter. Moreover, there was an absence of internal animosity to heighten the atmosphere. This would follow in part from the department's exclusion from the process of submitting proposals, but it may too have been to do with the fact that as the Head of Department was a non-graduate – like his staff – he was regarded by them as entirely outside the course of events and thus blameless.

As to the Science and Management Departments, a greater degree of agreement with the policy was to be expected, for two reasons. Firstly, both departments were involved in submitting degree course proposals and both departments had a number of graduates who would be well situated for involvement in such work if it was acquired. Secondly, in comparison with the Departments of Building and Engineering, they had only small amounts of low level work on their timetables.[11]

Part of the background to the first point is the high status of university education in this country.[12] In the educational world, the next best thing to a university lectureship is for one to be involved in degree work in a technical college. However, added to the status satisfaction to be derived

[10] Information given in an interview.

[11] cf. Chapter 3, Table 5.

[12] cf., for example, D. V. Glass, 'Education and Social Change in Modern England', in A. H. Halsey, etc. (eds.), *Education, Economy and Society*, New York, page 405 (1961).

from the college's acquisition of degree work for some lecturers, was perhaps the feeling that experience with such work at Jones College could act as a stepping stone to a post in a better institution. Indeed, some members of staff had admitted an interest in university posts. For instance, a scientist who supported the degree work policy said that he would 'like to teach in any university rather than a technical college'. Whilst a statistician, who also supported the policy, looked without enthusiasm at the prospect of spending the rest of his career in technical colleges and, when asked whether his ambition was to move into university teaching, replied:

'Well, that's rated equally with industry and both are put higher than a technical college.'

In their interviews respondents were asked whether they would like to teach in a university and of the fifteen who had been completely in favour of the degree work policy, nine said that they would whilst another two felt undecided about the idea.

However, it would be unwise to attribute the whole of the attraction of degree work to status; the intrinsic aspects of teaching at advanced levels were also, of course, important. A lawyer who had supported the policy had said on one occasion about the Management Department's most advanced courses (the HND and the Diploma of Management):

'The standard of the courses isn't high enough. For what I'm doing I'm overpaid.'

And the previously quoted statistician had said elsewhere:

'I'm teaching below capacity in content. I could easily teach at a higher level.'

Finally, for those members of staff involved with the college's advanced work rather than its junior work, a policy which was aimed at expanding the top end of the college carried with it the prospect of improved promotion prospects within the organisation.

The consequence of the relatively small proportions of low level work in the Science and Management Departments, to turn to the second point, was quite simply that there were fewer members of staff to fear the erosion of career prospects or, more radically, the need to transfer to a new college, should the proposals be successfully put into practice. Indeed, it was perhaps more likely that some of those involved in the junior work in these departments hoped to shed such work and to take over the more advanced, but sub-degree, work that their colleagues would leave behind them on their move into degree work.

87

Junior Work

In another open-ended question the staff were asked whether they agreed with the idea of transferring the college's lower level work to a new junior institution in the locality. The answers to this question are given in Table 18.

Table 18. Attitudes to the Transfer of
Lower Level Work[13]

In agreement	33
Ambivalent attitudes	2
Not in agreement	15
It depends on the future for higher level work	4
No opinion	2
Total	56*

* Question overlooked in the case of one respondent.

The most opposition, proportionately speaking, to the removal of low level work from the college came from members of the Engineering and Building Departments: of the fifteen responses expressing complete opposition to the idea nine came from members of these departments. On the other hand, only three of the twenty members of the Management Department interviewed expressed outright disapproval of the policy; these were members of the secretarial section of the department. Not one member of the Science Department interviewed felt that it was altogether wrong. The other three people who said that they were 'Not in agreement' with the plan were from the General Studies Department, but the balance of opinion was favourable to it in the department as a whole.[14] Table 19 gives the non-graduate/graduate breakdown of these answers. The policy's opponents tended to use economic and educational arguments in support of their position as with the degree work proposal.[15]

[13] Respondents were asked to define what they meant by 'low level' work and there was fairly general agreement that it was up to and including Ordinary National Certificate work.

[14] Seven people were in agreement, and the remaining person said it depended upon the future for higher level work.

[15] Similarly, no attempt was made to collect these answers systematically.

Table 19. Attitudes by Educational Qualifications of the Staff
to the Removal of Lower Level Work

	Non-graduates	Graduates
In agreement	17	16
Ambivalent attitudes	1	1
Not in agreement	12	3
It depends upon the future for higher level work	2	2
No opinion	0	2
Total	32	24

For example, a member of the Engineering Department felt that the consequence of such a policy would be that

'there would be nothing left for us to do. I think there is no justification, academically or economically, for it – there would be too many staff having too few hours'.

His colleague added,

'It would be more economical to take the higher level work away – because all the workshops exist for the lower level work.'[16]

A builder doubted whether the educational consequences of a junior college system of segregation would be desirable:

'I don't think it's a good thing: no. It's not a good thing from the students' or the staff viewpoint. From the teaching viewpoint you would find yourself teaching low level work all year round with no change, and from the students' viewpoint they would see all elementary work and no advanced work going on which they can get help from.'

A senior member of the Management Department's secretarial section put an allied point:

'I feel that it's very good for the younger people to be in an atmosphere where older people are working; it improves discipline, it makes them realise that they are little fish in a very big pond. And I honestly don't think their presence affects in any way the work done by more senior people on more senior courses.'

[16] Incidentally, this argument flatly contradicted that which the college had apparently used to the authorities over the issue of whether it should be responsible for the kind of basic training that was increasingly in demand consequent of the Industrial Training Act. *cf.* Chapter 3, page 39.

A General Studies Department lecturer argued that it seemed a retrograde step when modern thinking was in terms of comprehensive rather than segregated systems of education.

The supporters of the policy saw the situation in reverse. A junior member of the secretarial section, for example, said of the policy:

> 'I can't see that it would do any harm. Some people might argue that it is better for the lower level students to mix with the others, but I don't feel they do mix – they are not on the same wavelength as the other lot . . . I ask myself, "Would they work better?" And I think they would. Yet the problem is would they feel inferior, as in the case of secondary modern school pupils? I don't think they would so much with technical training.'

An ex-grammar school teacher in the General Studies Department was concerned more specifically with the discipline problems with regard to the junior students: 'The younger ones need a stronger discipline and don't get it.'

Whilst a lecturer in the Management Department felt that the junior students spoiled the atmosphere for the advanced students:

> 'It's not practical to have shorthand typists and gas boys being taught in the same place as degree equivalent work is going on. You don't get the right atmosphere.'

Again, whereas the opponents of the policy argued that they would be devoid of work if the low level courses were removed, some of its supporters felt that the place was cramped for space. For example, a scientist who was unsure of the merits of the policy in some ways nevertheless felt that the college was 'so overstretched for accommodation it may not be a bad thing'.[17]

As in the case of the degree work issue, we shall delve into the social and economic context of the junior college policy rather than rely upon such responses for our understanding of reaction to it. The college's action in showing itself willing to be rid of its low level work was probably deleterious for the status and self-esteem of those involved in this work in the college. Of course, given the valuation put upon the intelligent student and advanced education in our society,[18] the staff involved with the low level courses in Jones College could not enjoy the

---

[17] A member of the Engineering Department said he thought the transfer of work would 'help to relieve a lot of congestion'. A statistician from the Management Department remarked that 'if existing buildings can't be expanded then the feeder college was a good idea'.

[18] cf. D. V. Glass, op. cit. pages 402–403 and 405.

same status as their colleagues who taught on the more advanced ones. But the proposal to remove the low level work – in effect to say it was without value to the college – was to give it, and thereby the staff concerned, a definite hallmark of inferiority.

However, it was difficult to discern the extent to which the policy had brought about a greater sense of inferiority among some of the staff. Certainly, as has been seen, the secretarial staff had a markedly humble conception of their position in the college;[19] and a turn of phrase used by a builder and mentioned earlier,[20] 'It means the likes of us must go', gives the same impression that he regarded himself as less than equal. But to what extent such feelings were exacerbated by the junior college movement is difficult to say. One clearer indication of its effect is given by the comments of a member of the General Studies Department. He was leaving at the end of the year after having been with the college for four years – sufficient time in which to observe the effects of the policy. He had said:

> 'In this department there is general pessimism and low morale. The whole department is going downhill . . . The (junior college) business is one thing in the background.'[21]

It is possible that another indication of its effect was the incidence of nostalgia for the past. There was a nucleus of staff who had been with the college in its early days,[22] and among them one found references

[19] cf. Chapter 5, pages 72–73. Another secretarial teacher said, 'It's not a very elevated subject but it's nice to know you're helping them (the students) to earn a living at least.'

[20] cf. pages 85–86.

[21] His point is supported by the comments of other members of the department interviewed. See, for example, Chapter 5, pages 69–70. A Liberal Studies teacher also said, 'Our department is regarded as a general dogsbody: we have got to prove that it is providing a good service.'

[22] Twelve of the sample had been with the college for eight years or more. Their exact years of service were as follows:

Number of Years	Number of Staff	Comments
8	1	—
9	2	—
11	2	—
12	1	Originally part-time: full-time for 3 yr.
13	2	One person as above
14	2	—
18	2	One person originally part-time: full-time for 6 yr. Both started at Jones before the college was officially established.

being made to those days as preferable in some way.[23] It must be remembered that the early period of the college's history was one when low level work predominated in the timetable. This meant that not only were such staff on the whole drawn from the 'depressed' strata of the modern college, but also that they were looking back to a situation in which their own position was buoyant. A senior lecturer on the secretarial subjects side was a particular case in point: he had been with the college for fourteen years and in that time had helped to build up a section of considerable size. In the early days his position must have been surrounded with prestige; now his very existence in the college was being challenged. No wonder, therefore, that he should have said:

> 'The tendency in the last few years is to get away from the purpose, for which this college was built – full-time, part-time day and evening courses for the younger students.'

It follows from what has been said that an institution that was to be built upon the work rejected by Jones College would not enjoy the same status as the latter. That the new college would hold an inferior position is plainly recognised by one teacher of secretarial students whose comment on the policy was mentioned earlier.[24] She had asked herself, she said, whether the students in such a college would feel inferior, 'as in the case of secondary modern school pupils'.

A member of the General Studies Department revealed, in an informal conversation, that she was looking for another post in the area because she felt that her department was going to close down and she did not welcome the prospect of being transferred to a 'lower grade College'. Whilst a principal lecturer in the Management Department, when asked if he would be prepared to move to a new junior college, replied that there was a certain status level within the educational system beyond which he was not prepared to fall, and because of this he would not be willing to transfer.

Seen in these terms it was not to be expected that the junior college proposal would be regarded as attractive universally among the Jones

---

[23] For example, a member of the Building Department who had been at the college for eleven years replied to a question asking him whether he had noticed any changes in the college over the years as follows: 'There has been a breakdown in the connections between people in the departments. It was very pleasant when all the people who stayed in for lunch could sit round one table . . . there was a very communal set-up.' An engineer who had been there for thirteen years answered the same question as follows: 'Plenty. I used to know everybody on the staff down to the secretaries – there were only twenty-six of us.' Asked whether he liked it better then, he replied 'Much'.

[24] cf. page 90.

College staff. Nevertheless, it cannot be assumed that because the policy may have made the question of status more significant in the college than it had been before, it would be automatically rejected by everyone for whom it had unpleasant connotations. It was likely that some would feel that 'the issue having been raised' they could continue to stay at Jones College only under the condition of a poor relation status, and preferable to this was a transfer to the new college where they could enjoy parity of esteem. Certainly there were several respondents who supported the policy despite the fact that they were vulnerable to a transfer. Turning to its economic aspects, clearly for those who saw better prospects for themselves within Jones College as associated with the development of low level work (such as the welder previously quoted) [25] it would not be a welcome proposal.

Other members of staff, on the other hand, expressed the feeling that the junior work lowered the tone of Jones College. A principal lecturer in production management puts his point quite clearly:

> 'The trouble is that this place is such a mixture. You have women coming along here one afternoon to make cakes and then top level managers coming for courses. In the middle you have a lot of little boys and girls running around making love downstairs, etc. It makes it very difficult. You might hold a management conference for top level people and then they have to go and queue in the refectory for a cup of tea, and perhaps they find themselves standing behind their office boy.'

The desire to see the tone of the college improve has two aspects to it. Presumably, for some people the improvement was attractive for its own sake. But for others there was a more instrumental consideration. It was the association of the college with low level work that was thought to be at the bottom of its inability to obtain more advanced work. A comment of a scientist who had been enthusiastic both about the idea of degree work for the college and the transfer from it of the junior work is illustrative:

> 'Jones is so encumbered with low level work that it has affected the decision on the Polytechnic business.'

A principal lecturer in the same department, who also favoured the degree work proposal, declared that the junior work should have been moved five years before. Like his colleague he put the blame for the college's failure to achieve a firm foothold in the field of higher education on its association with junior work.

[25] *cf.* page 85.

93

The Character of the Work

The standard of the work to be aimed at was one of Jones College's goal problems. Another was the character of the work to be undertaken. In Chapter 2 some indication was given of the breadth of activity officially open to a college. This raised for the college the inter-related questions of what subjects to offer, what educational orientation to adopt and what markets to tap.

As it was, Jones College was a diverse institution in all these respects. A glance at its departmental structure alone[26] will show that it was an institution with a broad subject base. Moreover, it provided general education in the form of liberal studies and General Certificate of Education courses, training in specific skills such as welding, hairdressing and accountancy, and recreational facilities such as opportunities to make operas, to fence and to learn about photography. It advertised its courses in the national press and printed posters and brochures for local circulation. In this way it encouraged entry from members of the general public; but in addition, with the aid of circulars and conferences, firms were invited to tell the college about their specific needs.[27]

Our material on attitudes among the staff to this area of the college's goals is, unfortunately, of a haphazard nature. One reason for this was the failure to obtain in a usable form the information we had planned. But another was that it was only as the project proceeded that this aspect of the question of goals fully gained our attention. Despite its deficiencies, we have used this material below because it does indicate the dimensions of goal conflict and, more generally, amplifies the picture of the climate of the college that we have been attempting to construct.

General Education, Vocational Training and Recreation

One of the basic issues behind the questions of subjects and markets was that of whether a technical college was a place intended solely for vocational education and training or also for the continuation of general education.

We intended to obtain our information from the sample answers to a forced choice question on whether or not liberal studies should be included in the technical college's curriculum. In the event, this plan failed because respondents had difficulty in giving blanket answers of

[26] *cf.* Chapter 3, page 34.

[27] The section in the 1966–7 prospectus devoted to courses run by the Management Department contained the announcement that, 'In addition to the published programme, courses are arranged to meet the needs of particular companies and industries.'

this kind. What was obtained was six answers unfavourable to liberal studies, nineteen in favour and thirty-two containing qualified support, the qualifications covering such points as the age of the students, the length of their courses and the type of subjects to be taught. The restrictions placed on subject matter were sometimes so tight that the answers really amounted to unfavourable attitudes: for example, some respondents said that liberal studies should cover report writing and spelling or subjects related to their technical specialism. Although it was clear from these answers that enthusiasm for the idea of liberal studies varied, the nature and extent of the variation, unfortunately, remains somewhat confused. For example, some respondents probably appeared more (or less) favourably disposed than others towards liberal studies more because they were able to accept the convention of the forced choice question than because of their attitudes towards the issue itself.

The following comments illustrate the diversity of attitudes towards this subject:

> 'My ideas on liberal studies go back to the "Two Cultures". I think people should be aware that what others do is valuable. It's also got something to do with the cultivation of the "whole" man.'[28]
> 'The subjects should be completely divorced from a person's professional subject, but they should be a voluntary choice.'[29]
> 'Liberal Studies should be utilitarian, English rather than Liberal Studies, not too liberal. It should include things like report writing, letter writing, office procedures and speech training.'[30]
> 'If a firm finds it can release a student only one day a week then in fairness to the student and employers it should be used for technical training . . . The employer is paying you to do a particular job, he is not paying you to do liberal studies.'[31]
> 'If a college is a place of advanced or further education then it is not concerned with general knowledge, this is a school problem.'[32]

The place of liberal studies in courses designed basically to provide specific types of vocational training was one part of the issue. The other was whether the college should devote itself entirely to vocational work. The questionnaire included an open-ended question asking respondents to define the proper function of the college, but in

[28] An assistant lecturer in liberal studies. General Studies Dept.
[29] A senior lecturer, Science Department.
[30] An assistant lecturer, Science Department.
[31] A senior lecturer, Management and Business Studies Department.
[32] A lecturer in Production Management, Management and Business Studies Department.

the end we decided against using these answers for a conventional statistical table.[33] However, a few extracts from them are reproduced below in order to illustrate the different interpretations of the function of the college that existed among the staff. A production manager felt that the function of the college was 'to provide education to meet the requisites of industry and commerce,' and when he was asked whether he felt that this function was being carried out, he replied:

'By and large it is – most of the courses on our side of things have been sponsored by firms, very few are non-employed students.'

A senior lecturer in marketing felt that the college was not entirely fulfilling its proper function:

'It should just have been building, engineering and management.'

On the other hand, a lecturer in French felt that on the whole it was. She defined the college's function as follows:

'Firstly, it is to provide the opportunity to do the academic work that some people failed to do at school for some reason. Secondly, it is to enable people to do the things you can't do at school, like the management work and the catering work.'

A development of this debate over the relationship between vocational and general education was the question of where the college stood with regard to the provision of recreational facilities. Here again there was a marked divergence of opinions, for example:

'I think the tendency over the last year has been for there to be a swing to academic courses and the college has been trying to get rid of recreational courses. I think this is wrong because in ten years' time this college will have an important function in training for leisure.'[34]
'I should like housewives to come in for music appreciation, etc. . . . A lot of the so-called vocational courses are really just common sense, for instance, "management".[35]
'It should be the centre of things like that (i.e., recreational courses) if there's enough space, although the vocational should take precedence. But it's good to have some of that sort of work, to

[33] It was found that respondents needed a great deal of help with prompts.
[34] An assistant lecturer in English, General Studies Department.
[35] An assistant lecturer, General Studies Department.

96

play a part in local life. I think it could do a lot more, but it does well in putting on operas and things.'[36]

'Primarily the college should offer a service to people in a technical sense. A lot of space is taken up in the Women's Subjects block or, looking at my own department, in things like adult woodwork. It should be taken out because I don't think it's something that should be done in the college. The same thing applies to flower arrangements, art for beginners, etc.'[37]

'I think that facilities like judo and flower-arranging should be available, but not at Jones College.'[38]

The second issue was that of whom the college should regard as its clients. Was it there to serve the needs of firms or their employees whom they had released to attend the college?[39] This was by no means merely a conceptual point, as can be illustrated with the example of students sent to the college for an HND course in Business Studies by a firm of building contractors. This firm had stipulated that they did not wish the subject of marketing to be one of the optional subjects from which its students were to choose, yet some students had made it clear that this was a subject they were interested in taking.[40]

Staff attitudes on this issue were not explored. The indications are, however, that they would display the same differences as they displayed in the previous context, for at the same time as the Management Department was eagerly offering to 'tailor-made' courses for the individual firm or industry[41] and a member of that department was saying,

'The firms should be more serious about what they want. We create frustration, we teach people how to do things but either the firm doesn't take notice or the person is too low down to be taken notice of – I would rather have one manager than a dozen stock clerks in my class. I think the nature of my work should be selling ideas to top management and having more time for case study work in the firm itself. Just sending more students to colleges, if these are from the existing level, won't help.'

[36] A senior lecturer in statistics, Management and Business Studies Department.

[37] A lecturer, Building Department.

[38] A principal lecturer, Science Department.

[39] The issue was complicated by the fact that there was no legal compulsion upon employers to release employees to attend colleges. Thus it could be argued that the employer was the client.

[40] This was revealed in conversation with the researcher and by the fact that some of these students chose marketing as the subject of their extended essay, an examinable part of the course, and thereby tackled the subject on their own.

[41] The prospectus, *op. cit.*

An engineer was making the following complaint:

> 'Businessmen have far too much to say over courses. If they want
> a course put on then it is put on, yet this is taxpayers' money
> subsidising their courses.'

Conclusion

It has been shown that there was by no means a consensus of opinion
among the staff of Jones College on the standard of work with which
their college should be concerned. If the high level of calculative
involvement existed among the staff that has been suggested then
consensus was unlikely, for the economic and social implications of
policies towards advanced work and junior work varied with the
individual's position in the college.

It may have seemed, however, that we have overemphasised such
implications of these policies in our analysis of the determination of staff
attitudes towards them. That is, that we have exaggerated the importance
of such immediate utilitarian factors and undervalued the part played
by the staff's moral commitments – commitments to certain educational
ideologies. In our defence, we should point out that it was not merely
the researcher who saw the immediate utilitarian factors as of fundamental
importance: by their comments certain members of staff indicated that
they too felt the two issues at the college to be part of its climate of
careerism rather than a normative debate over educational goals. (Indeed
it may be that it was the activity surrounding the policies that had in
part evoked the feeling that careerism was characteristic of the college's
climate in the first place.)

An example of such an interpretation on the part of a member of the
staff has been provided already.[42] Further illustrations are given by the
the following quotations which refer to the degree work policy:

> 'I think it's the sign of a bit of ambitiousness on someone's part
> myself.'[43]
> 'For the most part the Management Department is full of chaps
> like myself, without qualifications. I think it was empire-building –
> most unsavoury.'[44]

[42] cf. the remark of the English and Liberal Studies teacher reproduced on page 83.
[43] An assistant lecturer, Engineering Department.
[44] A senior lecturer, General Studies Department.

'I think the purpose of a technical college is to serve the industry here and not the staff, and I think that was why they wanted the CNAA award.'[45]

The question of the character of the work the college should undertake was one with social and economic implications that also varied from individual to individual within the college. For the engineer who said,

'The public view of the technical college is one of an evening institute. The people either side of me here think that I teach evening hobbies: the public are not told enough about the trades side'[46]

the non-vocational work seemed to be merely an inconvenient drag on his image. But for the teacher of drama, or music, or physical education such work – that is, hobbies – was a bread and butter issue.
Having said this, it is probably true, however, that the reactions to the question of whether Jones College was a place for liberal studies and recreational work had a larger moral element in them than the reactions to most questions concerning goals. Apart from members of the General Studies Department[47] such work was not of fundamental importance for the careers of individuals. Where it was undertaken by members of the full-time staff outside this department it was usually done as a by-product of the person's main timetable. For example, a lecturer mainly concerned with the City and Guilds courses in carpentry might take an evening class in carpentry for women; or a chemist might volunteer to give a lecture or two on the philosophy of science in a liberal studies course. Thus there was greater room for feelings not associated with the individual's immediate career situation to enter into matters.
Returning to a point raised in the previous chapter – the genesis and development of group affiliations – it is possible to discern in the play of forces surrounding educational policy within the college, as described in this chapter, ways in which group feelings could either emerge or gain greater solidarity. For example, the members of the Science Department saw more to welcome in the degree work proposal than did members of the Engineering and Building departments, and the junior college proposal had more radical implications for those involved with the college's low level work than those involved with the more advanced work, and thus for non-graduates (except where the General Studies Department was concerned) than for graduates.

[45] A lecturer, Building Department.
[46] A reference to the respondent's neighbours.
[47] The Department of Catering, Fashion and Home Economics has been ignored, but it had more affinities with the General Studies Department with respect to the provision of recreational courses than any of the other departments in the college.

PART 3

7. Summary and Conclusions

Between 1951 and 1967 Jones College grew from a small institution
with under 3000 students and 13 full-time teaching staff into one with
over 12 000 students and 238 full-time teaching staff. If the growth of
the college is measured by the volume of its work rather than by student
numbers, then the picture is an even more dramatic one. Moreover, the
college changed in terms of the type of work in which it was involved as
well as in size. From being concerned mainly with low level courses for
students attending on a part-time basis, it reached a position where over
30 per cent of its student hours were attributed to 'university' level
work and 40 per cent of the total hours to full-time and sandwich
courses. The expansion in breadth of the college's work can be assessed
from the development of its departmental structure. It was to start the
1967–8 session with eight separate departments: in 1952 there were
only three, and it is doubtful whether in the year prior to that any such
division of the work had been made at all. This growth in the number
of departments illustrates, too, the college's organisational complexity
in its later stage.

To some extent, official policy on further education provides an explanation
for the development of the college. It provided, in the early days, a
permissive climate for the further education sector and even later on its
attitude was marked more by ambiguities and loop-holes than
authoritarianism. Similarly, the market environment of Jones College
must also be credited with a large share of responsibility for shaping the
college, its willingness to take advantage of the courses supplied by the
college was of course an essential factor. But neither offical policy nor
the market can fully explain why the college enrolled students at the rate
at which it did enrol them and selected the particular courses to offer to
the market that it did select.

Examination of college documents, coupled with information supplied
by members of the college, revealed that Jones College had a history
of attempts to surmount official restrictions on course development,
and that it was not averse to running down its courses even when they
were enthusiastically supported by the market or energetically pushing
courses for which demand was dubious or to which other institutions
were laying claim. Such characteristics were scarcely those of an institution
playing a passive part in its own development.

The structure and climate of the college emanated from its particular
course of development and can be understood only against such a
background. But at the same time they, the structure and climate of
interaction, influenced the development of the college. The diffuseness

of official goals made it possible for Jones College to acquire a multiplicity of educational functions: this brought into the college as teachers people with widely differing educational and occupational backgrounds.

Factors that could have stood for or promoted a sense of group identity among these teachers were particularly lacking. The possibility that they were attracted to the college initially by some sense of common purpose is doubtful because the image of the technical college in our society is relatively indistinct. The extent of the opportunity for common experiences among them subsequently was limited for two reasons at least. Firstly, few of the members of Jones College had undergone a full course of training for teaching in further education and, secondly, the work situation in the college was characterised by variation in the nature and level of the teaching and the physical separation of people by staggered timetables and the layout of buildings. The growth of a group identity was hampered in another way: as we have said, the size of the full-time teaching staff expanded yearly. At the same time, however, the college was losing teachers. Between 1953 and 1965 the annual turnover rate never dropped below 7·4 per cent, averaged 11·5 per cent, and reached 17·2 per cent.[1] This means that for the total staff to have steadily increased despite a constant outflow of people, the proportion of new faces to appear among the staff each year had to be quite considerable. Such a process would not have encouraged the establishment and maintenance of a special college ethos.

Indeed, the work situation was probably positively divisive in its effect and for other reasons as well. There was the process of departmentalisation to create separate foci of allegiance. There was also the attitudes engendered by the college's history of change: it seems as if, because the college had a history of constant growth and change, staff had come to look upon change as a normal condition of life in Jones College and to have developed heightened sensibilities to the relationships between educational

---

[1] The full details of the staff turnover rates, calculated from the annual list of names printed in the college prospectus, are as follows:

Year	Rate* %	Year	Rate %	Year	Rate %
1953–4	7·4	1958–9	9·9	1962–3	12·8
1954–5	10·5	1959–60	12·3	1963–4	11·4
1955–6	17·2	1960–1	12·7	1964–5	7·4
1956–7	11·3	1961–2	16·6	1965–6	13·1
1957–8	7·5				

* This is the percentage of full-time teaching staff employed at the beginning of the year, who left during the year.

courses and its future states. This meant that courses taught on or planned by some members of staff were construed by others as either threats or hindrances to their own future positions.

With the combination of pre-college and college experiences there was the potential for a complicated network of relationships among the staff. For example, we established three sets of inter-related identities: namely, departmental membership, and being with or without a degree and with or without industrial experience.

The attitudes of members of staff to their work were, of course, important for the climate of the college. Although different in so many ways, the staff did have at least one factor to some extent in common; they had a tendency to use extrinsic characteristics of further education teaching, such as conditions of service and prospects, to explain why they had chosen to enter the field, rather than such intrinsic factors as the desire to teach or to perform a useful function in society. The low incidence among them of training for teaching in further education seems to verify the conclusion that they had been motivated to enter the job more by calculative than moral factors.

The college working conditions were such that it seems doubtful whether they gave these teachers sufficient opportunity for deriving intrinsic satisfaction from their work, or developing moral commitment to it, to allow such calculative attitudes the chance to diminish.[2] The mechanics of the teaching situation made teaching necessarily more repetitive and the teacher-student relationship more superficial than they have to be elsewhere in the educational system.[3] Moreover, the facilities for research were not good.

Administration was an important feature of the work of some Jones College teachers and a certain number of such non-teaching tasks were carried out by all members of staff. Their attitude to this aspect of the technical college teacher's job was interesting: it was found that, instead of strongly objecting to the intrusion of non-teaching tasks into their role, on the whole members accepted such tasks with equanimity if not with pleasure. This seemed to be an indication of the continuation of a low level of moral commitment to teaching and also a sign of the lack of intrinsic satisfaction to be derived from it among the staff.

Here then, in our opinion, was a collection of people who neither worked for an institution with a special and cherished image[4] nor were

[2] *cf.* Chapter 4, page 57.
[3] *cf.* Introduction, page 12, for B. Wilson's point about the conflict between commitment to pupils and a career orientation.
[4] An example of people who do is teachers in a Grammar School with a good reputation. These normally object to 'going comprehensive'.

held tightly together by bonds of special understanding and mutual interests, who appeared to have quite a strong calculative orientation to their work and to be relatively untrammelled by a moral commitment to teaching. This particular assortment of structural and motivational characteristics would appear to be especially conducive to the growth and change of an educational institution.

It is interesting to reflect upon the possible part played by the factor of administration in the college's development in this context. It was popularly believed by the Jones College staff that administration was important as a lever for promotion. If this was in fact so, here was a particular factor stimulating the growth and change of the college: for administration was intimately associated with the task of running courses. The simplest way for a member of staff to demonstrate his administrative expertise was for him to sponsor or run a new course. There is logic in such a system of promotion which suggests that this belief was rooted quite firmly in the actual circumstances. The more senior a member of staff's position in the college's hierarchy of authority the less teaching and the more administrative tasks he is time-tabled to do. Thus the successful candidate for promotion had to show not so much that he was a good teacher but that he possessed a capacity for the new administrative tasks that he would have to carry out. And indeed we have reproduced comments of senior members of the college which confirm that they looked for or were attracted by such capacities in their staff.

We have said that the structural characteristics and the climate of the college were both the product of the college's particular course of development and a source of its momentum for further growth and change. However, members of staff were demonstrably not alike in their interests, or personal goals, and these interests sometimes required incompatible college states for their satisfaction. Thus, given that the college could pursue only one course of development at a time, it was impossible for members of staff to have played equally influential parts in its actual or projected development. The ability of individual members to exercise their influence in this way, and to satisfy their personal goals through the college, would depend upon the relationship of these goals to such factors as the goals of superiors in the college, official policy towards further education and the market situation. What the history of Jones College shows is that those members of staff who were enthusiastic about advanced work stood particularly good chances of having the sympathetic ear of a Head of Department, and without this individual members of staff were powerless.

This study of Jones College contains a number of points that are of relevance for organisational analysis more generally. The concept of the organisational goal will be taken first of all. It shows, firstly, that to look upon the organisational goal as something specific in character is inadequate.[5] Official policy towards the technical college was both vague and diffuse, and to make sense of what the individual college acted on it was necessary to think in terms of Perrow's official and operative goals.[6] Secondly, it makes evident the fact that operative goals can subvert official goals just as much as they can support them. Ambiguous though the letter of official policy was after 1956, there was little doubt that in spirit it was against the unnecessary proliferation of advanced work in area colleges. Yet Jones College pursued such work under dubious market conditions fairly relentlessly. Thirdly, it illustrates operative goals in conflict. Members of Jones College variously wanted the college to be an institution devoted to, or more devoted to, advanced work, low level work, industry oriented courses, general education, young school-leavers and to mature workers.

Fourthly, it provides support for Albrow's point that

'the notion of the specific goal as the origin and cause of the organisation is an unhistorical myth'.[7]

He is criticising those definitions of organisations that suggest an organisation comes into being because a number of people come together motivated by a common purpose, a purpose which they are unable to achieve singly. Such a view, he says, ignores the fact that goals arise in the course of an organisation's development rather than in the form of a 'specific "common" purpose' and 'minimises the importance of constraint' in the setting of goals.[8] Jones College indeed acquired its functions in a haphazard fashion over time and contained people at many levels who were entirely opposed to the direction that the college had been taking but who were powerless to prevent it from doing so. Fifthly, although official policy towards technical colleges provides a good illustration of a lack of specificity in the setting of official goals, it also shows that although official goals may start life as vague notions they can increase in clarity. For the technical college structure became increasingly more closely defined between 1944 and 1966. Perrow's definitions, for all their merits as analytical tools, do contain a danger. They do suggest a static approach to official goal-setting. What seems to have happened in this field is that a process of inter-action between

---

[5] *cf.* Introduction, pages 5–7.
[6] *Ibid,* page 7.
[7] M. Albrow, *op. cit.* page 153.
[8] M. Albrow, *op. cit.,* page 160.

official and operative goals took place, with the former going through reformulations partly on cues from the latter. Educational policy makers, seeing the expansionary results of earlier recommendations, tightened up the technical college system by providing its various sectors with more precisely defined areas of operation.

Turning from a consideration of goals to a consideration of structure, the history of Jones College also indicates the validity of approaching formal structure as a product of organisational development rather than as something necessarily laid down at the time the enterprise comes into being.[9] The fundamental part of Jones College's formal organisation was its pattern of departments and its staff hierarchy. Both of these evolved out of the college's growth and the particular educational functions it acquired. There could have been no knowledge at the start that Jones College would grow to such an extent that it could support eight departments and 238 full-time members of staff, nor that particular subjects would be present in the way they came to be present – that there would be a Department of Mathematics and Computing and a Senior Lectureship in Purchasing, for example. We have argued that the growth of the college and the disposition of its courses has to be seen partly as the product of internal forces. Therefore, we must also argue that this formal structure was in part thrown up from below, influenced by the activities of ordinary members of staff.

Indeed, Jones College illustrates what happens when the formal structure is capable of being changed, is visibly responsive to the activities of ordinary members of staff. It was this characteristic that contributed to the use of epithets such as careerism and empire-building by some members of staff to describe the activities of their colleagues, and to the complaints that the atmosphere of the college was competitive. The atmosphere felt competitive because success came not only in the form of promotion into 'dead men's shoes' but also as self-made new positions in the hierarchy, and failure therefore meant not just non-promotion but a re-structured hierarchy in which old positions could be vulnerable.

Our final point is a reflection on social control. Much has been written about the differences between bureaucratic and professional modes of social control.[10] In the former case the source of control is said to be vested in the hierarchy of authority and in the latter in internalised codes of ethics and peer group sanctions. A technical college appears to occupy that fairly common position of being an organisation containing

[9] *cf.* Introduction, pages 7–9.
[10] *cf.*, for example, P. Blau and W. R. Scott, *op. cit.* pages 62–63, and A. Etzioni, *Modern Organizations,* New Jersey, pages 76–77 (1964), although Etzioni prefers to talk about an 'administrative' system rather than a bureaucratic one.

characteristics of both bureaucratic and professional structures.[11] Jones College, with its formal pyramid-shaped staff hierarchy headed by the Principal with responsibility for 'day-to-day management and discipline',[12] and its freedom for staff over their teaching and the planning of courses, illustrated that these two orientations were, so to speak, structurally present.

However, it seems doubtful whether the methods of social control that we associate with the professional model would operate effectively in the Jones College environment. The members of staff lacked a common base of knowledge, coming as they did into teaching from many walks of life and to carry out different educational tasks, and thus they were not in ideal positions to pass expert judgments upon one another. They also lacked common training for teaching and therefore had no opportunity to internalise a common code of ethics, should one in fact exist. What is more, they undoubtedly had different reference groups, and for this reason it seems unlikely that the college peer group, or technical college teachers as a whole, would constitute an effective source of normative control.[13] For example, how could members of the college effectively reproach a colleague who pushed forward plans for degree courses regardless of the need for them when he did so to improve his chances of obtaining a university lectureship?

Thus Jones College appears to provide an example of an organisational situation lacking in a complete system of bureaucratic controls and

[11] cf. P. Blau and W. R. Scott, op. cit. pages 64–73, and Etzioni, op. cit. pages 78–79.

[12] Ministry of Education, Governing Bodies for Major Establishments of Further Education, Circular 7/59, 10 August 1959.

[13] Of interest in this context is Gouldner's distinction between cosmopolitans and locals. In his study of an American liberal arts college, Gouldner differentiated between two types of organisational roles with the variables loyalty to the organisation, commitment to professional or specialised skills and values, and reference group orientation. Cosmopolitans were those people found to be relatively low on loyalty, high on professional commitment and using an outer reference group orientation, whilst locals were those people who were relatively high on loyalty, low on professional commitment and using an inner reference group orientation. Some of the characteristics selected as indications of these orientations were clearly in evidence among the members of Jones College. For example, cosmopolitans more often than locals wanted lighter work loads so as to have more time for private research, found the college deficient in people with whom they could share their professional interests, had publications credited to them and would readily leave the college for another. However, the Jones College situation was especially complex because outer reference groups could be not only academic circles but also industry and schools. (cf. Alvin W. Gouldner, 'Cosmopolitans and Locals: Towards an Analysis of Latent Social Roles', Administrative Science Quarterly, 2, pages 281–306, 444–480 (1957–8).

containing conditions unpropitious for the operation of supplementary, or complementary, professional controls.

Ideally, the next step is to find out the extent to which Jones College is typical of post-war technical colleges. It is hoped that more studies of colleges will be undertaken to permit comparisons to be made. In such studies, moreover, it would be desirable to see treated in greater depth those things which here have been merely touched upon in our process of exploration. For example, more needs to be known about the social identities among members of staff and their meaning for a college[14] and about the relationships between colleges and their governing bodies, local authorities, other local educational institutions and business firms.

[14] For example, Gouldner (*op. cit.*) goes on to investigate the differences between cosmopolitans and locals in terms of their participation in college activities, attitudes to its rules and regulations, degrees of influence and informal relations.

References in Text

Books and Articles

Albrow, M., 'The Study of Organizations – Objectivity or Bias?', in Gould, J. (ed.), *Penguin Social Sciences Survey, 1968,* Harmondsworth: Penguin Books, pages 146–167 (1968).

Anon., 'Ignorance of the "Tech",' *Technical Education,* June, page 248 (1966).

Argles, M., *South Kensington to Robbins,* London: Longmans (1964).

Banks, O., *The Sociology of Education,* London, Batsford (1968).

Bernstein, B., 'Open Schools, Open Society?', *New Society,* 14 September, pages 351–353 (1967).

Blau, P., and Scott, W. R., *Formal Organizations,* London, Routledge & Kegan Paul (1966), paperback edition (first published 1963).

Brosan, G. S., 'The Government of Technical Colleges', a paper given to the 1966 National Educational Conference, available in typescript from the Association of Teachers in Technical Institutions.

Cantor, L. M. and Roberts, I., *Further Education in England and Wales,* London: Routledge & Kegan Paul (1969).

Clark, B. R., *The Open Door College,* New York: McGraw-Hill (1960).

Cotgrove, S., *Technical Education and Social Change,* London: Routledge & Kegan Paul (1958).

Cotgrove, S., 'Education and Occupation', *The British Journal of Sociology,* **13,** 1, pages 33–42 (1962).

Etzioni, A., 'The Organizational Structure of "Closed" Educational Institutions in Israel', *Harvard Educational Review,* **27,** pages 107–125 (1957).

Etzioni, A., 'Two Approaches to Organizational Analysis: a Critique and a Suggestion', *Administrative Science Quarterly,* **5,** 2, pages 257–278 (1960).

Etzioni, A., *A Comparative Analysis of Complex Organizations,* Glencoe, Ill.: The Free Press (1961).

Etzioni, A., *Modern Organizations,* New Jersey: Prentice-Hall (1964).

Gerth, H. H. and Mills, C. W. (trs. and eds.), *From Max Weber,* New York: Oxford University Press (1958), paperback edition.

Glass, D. V., 'Education and Social Change in Modern England', in Halsey, A. H., Floud, J. and Anderson, C. A. (eds.), *Education, Economy and Society,* Glencoe, Ill.: Free Press, pages 391–413 (1961).

Glennerster, H. and Pryke, R., 'The Public Schools', *Young Fabian Pamphlet* (1964).

Goffman, E., *Asylums,* New York: Doubleday (1961).

Gouldner, A. W., 'Cosmopolitans and Locals: Toward an Analysis of Latent Social Roles', *Administrative Science Quarterly,* **2,** pages 281–306 and 444–480 (1957–8).

Hoyle, E., 'Organizational Analysis in the Field of Education', *Educational Research,* **7,** pages 97–114 (1965).

Junker, B. H., *Field Work. An Introduction to the Social Sciences,* Chicago: University of Chicago Press (1960).

Klein, V., 'Working Wives', *Occasional Paper No. 15,* Institute of Personnel Management (1959).

Klein, V., *Britain's Married Women Workers,* London: Routledge & Kegan Paul (1965).

Lambert, R., 'The Public Schools, a Sociological Introduction', in Kalton, G., *The Public Schools,* London: Longmans, pages xi–xxxii (1966).

March, J. G. and Simon, H. A., *Organizations,* New York: Wiley (1958).

Millerson, G., *The Qualifying Associations ,* London: Routledge & Kegan Paul (1964).

Mouzelis, N. P., *Organisations and Bureaucracy,* London: Routledge & Kegan Paul (1967).

Musgrave, P. M., *Technical Change, the Labour Force and Education,* Oxford: Pergamon (1967).

Perrow, C., 'The Analysis of Goals in Complex Organizations', *American Sociological Review,* **26,** 6, pages 854–866 (1961).

Peters, A. J., *British Further Education,* Oxford: Pergamon (1967).

Robinson, E., *The New Polytechnics,* Harmondsworth: Penguin (1968).

Selznick, P., *TVA and the Grass Roots,* Berkeley: The University of California (1949).

Selznick, P., *The Organizational Weapon,* Glencoe, Ill.,: The Free Press (1962) (first published 1952).

Selznick, P., *Leadership in Administration,* Evanston, Ill.: Row, Peterson (1957).

Silverman, D. *The Theory of Organisations,* London: Heinemann (1970).

Sofer, C. and Hotton, G., *New Ways in Management Training,* London: Tavistock Publications (1958).

Thompson, V., 'Hierarchy, Specialization and Organizational Conflict', *Administrative Science Quarterly,* **5,** 1961.

Tipton, B. F. A., 'Some Organisational Characteristics of a Technical College', *Research in Education,* **7,** May, pages 11–27 (1972).

Venables, E., *The Young Worker at College,* London: Faber & Faber (1967).

Venables, P., 'The Demand for Technical Education in the United Kingdom', *The World Year Book of Education, 1965,* London: Evans (1965).

Wall, W. D., 'Educational Research in Technical Colleges', a paper given to the 1966 National Educational Conference, available in typescript from the Association of Teachers in Technical Institutions.

Weinberg, I., *The English Public Schools,* New York: Atherton Press (1967).

Wilson, B., 'The Teacher's Role – a Sociological Analysis', *The British*

Journal of Sociology, **13**, 1, pages 15–32 (1962).
Wilson, J., *Public Schools and Private Practice,* London: Allen &
Unwin (1962).

Official Documents (chronologically)

Education Act, 1944.
Ministry of Education, *Education in 1952,* HMSO, Cmnd. 8835 (1953);
Technical Education, HMSO Cmnd. 9703 (1956) (White Paper);
Education in 1957, HMSO Cmnd. 454 (1958);
Central Advisory Council for Education, *15 to 18,* 1, HMSO (1959)
(Crowther Report).
Ministry of Education, *Better Opportunities in Technical Education,*
HMSO, Cmnd. 1254 (1961) (White Paper); *Forward From School,*
HMSO (1962).
Ministry of Education and Department of Education and Science,
Statistics of Education, Part Two, for 1963, 1964 and 1965, HMSO,
1964, 1965 and 1966.
Committee on Higher Education, *Higher Education Report,* HMSO,
Cmnd. 2154 (1963) (Robbins Report).
Report by a Sub-Committee of the National Advisory Council on
Education for Industry and Commerce, *The Public Relations of Further
Education* (1964).
Committee on Technical College Resources, *Report on the Size of Classes
and Approval of Further Education Courses* (1966) (Pilkington Report).
Department of Education and Science, *A Plan for Polytechnics and Other
Colleges,* HMSO, Cmnd. 3006 (1966) (White Paper).
University Grants Committee, *University Development 1972–67,* HMSO,
Cmnd. 3820 (1968).

In addition the following Ministry of Education and Department of
Education and Science Circulars and Administrative Memoranda for the
period 1945–1966 have been referred to:

Circulars

56	*Further Education – Some Immediate Problems*
94	*Research in Technical Colleges*
109	*Training for the Catering Industry*
117	*Further Education Homecraft*
133	*Schemes of Further Education and Plans for County Colleges*
139	*Plan for County Colleges*
255	*Advanced Technology*

270   *Advanced Short Courses for Scientists and Technologists Engaged in Industry*
305   *The Organisation of Technical Colleges*
323   *Liberal Education in Technical Colleges*
1/59   *Technical Education – The Next Step*
5/59   *Further Education for Commerce*
7/59   *Governing Bodies for Major Establishments of Further Education*
1/60   *The Future Development of Management Education and Business Studies*
3/61   *Regional Colleges*
3/63   *Organisation of Further Education Courses*
7/63   *Management Education*
14/64   *The Henniker-Heaton Report on Day Release*
2/66   *Management Studies in Technical Colleges*
11/66   *Technical College Resources: Size of Classes and Approval of Classes and Approval of Further Education Courses*

Administrative Memoranda

7/61   *National Certificates and Diplomas in Business Studies*
6/62   *Forward from School*
4/64   *The Industrial Training Act, 1964*

A Selection from other Works Consulted

General

Argyris, C., *Integrating the Individual and the Organizations*, New York: Wiley (1964).

Bakke, E. W., 'Concept of the Social Organization' in M. Haire (ed.), *Modern Organization Theory, op. cit.* pages 16–75.

Barrett, F. D., 'The Staff-Line Dilemma', *Executive*, June (1964), pages 45–47.

Blau, P. M., *Bureaucracy in Modern Society*, New York: Random House (1956).

Broom, L. and Selznick, P., *Sociology*, New York: Harper & Row, third edition (1963).

Bruyn, S. T., *The Human Perspective in Sociology: The Methodology of Participant Observation*, New Jersey: Prentice-Hall (1966).

Burns, T. and Stalker, G. M., *The Management of Innovation*, London: Tavistock (1961).

Clark, P. B. and Wilson, J. Q., 'Incentive Systems a Theory of Organizations', *Administrative Science Quarterly*, **6**, 2, pages 129–166 (1961).

Coleman, J. S., 'Relational Analysis: The Study of Social Organizations with Survey Methods', in A. Etzioni (ed.), *Complex Organizations, op. cit.* pages 441–464.

Eisenstadt, S. N., 'Bureaucracy and Bureaucratization', *Current Sociology*, **7**, pages 97–164 (1958).

Etzioni, A., 'Administration and the Consumer', *Administrative Science Quarterly*, **3**, 2, pages 251–264 (1958).

Etzioni, A., 'Authority Structure and Organizational Effectiveness', *Administrative Science Quarterly*, **4**, 1, pages 43–67 (1959).

Etzioni, A., (ed.), *Complex Organizations: A Sociological Reader*, New York: Holt (1961).

Georgopoulos, B. S. and Tannenbaum, A. S., 'A Study of Organizational Effectiveness', *American Sociological Review*, **22**, 5, pages 534–540 (1957).

Gouldner, A. W., *Patterns of Industrial Bureaucracy*, Glencoe, III: Free Press (1954).

Gouldner, A. W., 'Organizational Analysis', in R. J. Merton (ed.), *Sociology Today*, New York: Basic Books (1959).

Grusky, O., 'Career Mobility and Organizational Commitment', *Administrative Science Quarterly*, **10**, 4, pages 486–503 (1966).

Gusfield, J. R., 'Occupational Roles and Forms of Enterprise', *American Journal of Sociology*, **66**, 6, pages 571–580 (1961).

Haire, M. (ed.), *Modern Organization Theory*, New York: Wiley (1959).

Jaques, E., *The Changing Culture of a Factory*, London: Tavistock, second impression (1952).

113

Litwak, E., 'Models of Bureaucracy which Permit Conflict', *American Journal of Sociology,* **67,** 2, pages 177–184 (1961).

Merton, R. K. *et al.* (eds.), *Reader in Bureaucracy,* Glenco, Ill.: Free Press (1952).

Parsons, T., 'Suggestions for a Sociological Approach to the Theory of Organizations – I and II', *Administrative Science Quarterly,* **1,** 1 and 2, pages 63–85 and pages 224–239 (1956).

Perrow, C., 'Organizational Prestige: Some Functions and Dysfunctions', *American Journal of Sociology,* **66,** 4, pages 335–341 (1961).

Rex, J., *Key Problems in Sociological Theory,* London: Routledge & Kegan Paul (1961).

Selznick, P. 'Foundations of the Theory of Organization', *American Sociological Review,* **13,** pages 25–35 (1948).

Simon, H. A., 'On the Concept of Organizational Goal', *Administrative Science Quarterly,* **9,** 1 pages 1–22 (1964).

Thompson, J. D. and McEwen, W. J., 'Organizational Goals and Environment: Goal-Setting as an Interaction Process', *American Sociological Review,* **23,** 1, pages 23–31 (1958).

Van Doorn, J. A. A., 'Conflict in Formal Organizations', in A. de Reuch and J. Knight (eds.), *Conflict in Society,* London: Churchill, pages 111–132 (1966).

Whyte, W. F., *Street Corner Society,* University of Chicago, revised edition (1955).

Whyte, W. H., Jr., *The Organization Man,* New York: Simon & Schuster (1956).

Wilensky, H. L., 'The Professionalization of Everyone?', *American Journal of Sociology,* **70,** 2, pages 137–158 (1964).

Education

Anon., 'What are "Techs" for?', *Times Review of Industry and Technology,* **3,** 8 (1965).

Anon., 'The Drift from the Schools', *Technical Education,* page 99, March (1966).

Anon., 'Colleges May Be Divided into Haves and Have Nots', *Times Educational Supplement,* page 1125, 7 April (1967).

Anon., 'The Laboratory Technician', *New Left Review,* **46,** pages 55–62, November–December (1967).

Armstrong, B., 'Responsibility for New Staff in Colleges . . . 2', *Technical Education,* pages 16–18, January (1966).

Baron, G., *A Bibliographical Guide to the English Educational System,* London: Athlone, third edition (1965).

Baron, G. and Tropp, A., 'Teachers in England and Wales', in A. H. Halsey, *et al.* (eds.), *Education, Economy and Society, op. cit.* pages 545–557.

Bennis, W. G., 'The Effect on Academic Goods of Their Market', *American Journal of Sociology,* **62,** pages 28–33 (1956).

Clark, B. R., 'Organizational Adaptation and Precarious Values: A Case Study', *American Sociological Review,* **21,** 3, pages 327–336 (1956).

Clark, B. R., *Educating the Expert Society,* California: Chandler (1962).

Clark, B. R., 'Interorganizational Patterns in Education', *Administrative Science Quarterly,* **10,** 2, pages 224–237 (1965).

Cotgrove, S., 'The Administration of Academics', *The Technical Journal,* pages 20–22, July (1967).

Geer, B. 'Occupational Commitment and the Teaching Profession', *The School Review,* **74,** 1, pages 31–47 (1966).

Getzels, J. and Guba, E., 'The Structure of Roles and Role Conflict in the Teaching Situation', *Journal of Education Sociology,* **29,** pages 30–40 (1955).

Gordon, C. W., 'The Role of the Teacher in the Social Structure of the High School', *ibid.* pages 21–29.

Gross, N. and Heriott, R., *Staff Leadership in Public Schools: A Sociological Inquiry,* New York: Wiley (1965).

Hansbury, J., 'Technical Teaching – Vocation or Profession ?', *Technical Education,* pages 22–26, January (1966).

Leese, J., 'A New Voice for Further Education', *Technical Education,* pages 298–300, July (1966).

Leese, J., 'Tertiary Education and Local Government', *Technical Education & Industrial Training,* **9,** 2, pages 66–68 (1967).

Liepmann, K., *Apprenticeship,* London: Routledge & Kegan Paul (1960)

Rourke, F. E. and Brooks, G. E., 'The Managerial Revolution in Higher Education', *Administrative Science Quarterly,* **9,** 2, pages 154–181 (1964).

Silberston, D., *Youth in a Technical Age: A Study of Day Release,* London: Parrish (1959).

Silver, H., 'Education and the Working of Democracy', *Technical Education,* pages 268–269, June (1966).

Stevens, F., *The Living Tradition: the Educational and Sociological Assumptions of the Grammar School,* London: Hutchinson (1960).

Taylor, W., *The Secondary Modern School,* London: Faber (1964).

Terrien, F., 'The Occupational Roles of Teachers', *Journal of Educational Sociology, op. cit.* pages 14–20.

Tropp, A., 'The Changing Status of Teachers in England and Wales', in *Year Book of Education,* London: Evans, pages 147–170 (1953).

Venables, P. F. R., *Technical Education,* London: Bell (1955).
Waller, W., *The Sociology of Teaching,* New York: Wiley (1965 edition).
Webb, J., 'The Sociology of a School', *British Journal of Sociology,* **13,** 3, pages 264–272 (1962).
Wellens, J., 'The Technical College in a Changing Environment', *Technical Education,* pages 444–447 October, (1965).
Wheeler, G. E., 'The Management of Colleges', *Technical Journal,* **4,** 4, pages 8–11 (1966).
Wilkinson, R., *The Prefects,* Oxford University Press (1964).
Williams, G., *Recruitment to Skilled Trades,* London: Routledge & Kegan Paul (1957).

Official and Other Reports, etc.

(*i*) *Official*

Board of Education/Ministry of Education/Department of Education and Science, Annual Education Reports for 1937 and then 1947 onwards, Monthly 'Reports on Education' from July 1963, Circulars and Administrative Memoranda 1945–67.
Ministry of Education, *Further Education,* Pamphlet No. 8, HMSO (1947).
Report of a Special Committee Appointed by the Ministry of Education, *Education for Management,* HMSO (1947) (Urwick Report).
Report of a Special Committee on Education for Commerce, HMSO (1949) (Carr-Saunders Report).
National Advisory Council on Education for Industry and Commerce, *The Future Development of Higher Technological Education,* HMSO (1950) (Weeks Report).
Ministry of Education, *Higher Technological Education,* HMSO, Cmnd. 8357 (1951) (White Paper).
Advisory Council on Scientific Policy and Ministry of Labour, *Scientific and Engineering Manpower in G.B.,* HMSO (1956) (Zuckerman Report).
Report of a Special Committee, *The Supply and Training of Teachers for Technical Colleges,* HMSO (1957) (Willis Jackson Report).
National Advisory Council on Education for Industry and Commerce, *Report of the Advisory Committee on Further Education for Commerce,* HMSO (1958) (McMeeking Report).
National Advisory Council on Education for Industry and Commerce, *Report on the Wastage of Students from Part-time Technical and Commercial Courses,* HMSO (1959).
National Advisory Council on Training and Supply of Teachers, *Teachers for Further Education,* HMSO (1961) (Russell Report).

Ministry of Education, *General Studies in Technical Colleges,* HMSO (1962).
United Kingdom Advisory Council on Education and Management, *Management Studies in Technical Colleges,* HMSO (1962) (Platt Report).
Industrial Training: Government Proposals, HMSO, Cmnd. 1892 (1962) (White Paper).
National Advisory Council on Education for Industry and Commerce, *Report of the Advisory Sub-Committee on Sandwich Courses,* HMSO (1963) (Russell Report).
Report of a Special Committee of the Minister of Education on Day Release, HMSO (1964) (Henniker-Heaton Report).
National Advisory Council on Education for Industry and Commerce, *A Higher Award for Business Studies,* HMSO (1964) (Crick Report).
United Kingdom Advisory Council in Education and Management, *Management Studies in Technical Colleges,* HMSO (1965) (2nd Platt Report).
National Advisory Council on the Training and Supply of Teachers, *The Supply and Training of Teachers for Further Education,* HMSO (1966) (Russell Report).
Department of Education and Science and Central Office of Information, *Further Education for School Leavers,* HMSO (1966).

(ii) Other
A Report of a Conference of Representatives of the Associations of LEAs and the LCC, *Co-operation in Technical Education,* HMSO (1937).
Association of Principals of Technical Institutions, *Policy in Technical Education,* Summer Meeting 10–12 June 1954.
Association of Technical Institutions, 'Whither Technical Education?' by J. T. Drakoley, *Annual Summer Meeting,* 23–24 June, 1930.
A.T.T.I., Policy statements and other publications, 1962 onwards.
Federation of British Industries Technical College Committee, *The Technical Colleges and their Government: An Industrial Appraisal* (1960).
National Association of Schoolmasters Committee for Technical Education, *Educational Objectives in Further Education* (1963).

Appendix I

Student Hours: 1951–2–1966–7

Year	Full-time	Sandwich	Short Courses	Part-time day	Evenings	Total	Growth
1951	4866	—	—	134 756*	138 332†	277 954	100·0
1952	43 730	—	—	160 626*	167 598†	371 954	133·8
1953	45 980	—	—	176 502*	196 803†	459 285	165·2
1954	93 903	—	—	198 159*	206 918†	498 980	179·5
1955	119 183	—	—	232 666*	245 004†	598 653	215·4
1956	142 914	—	—	270 699*	270 918†	684 531	246·3
1957							
1958	269 352	—	—	367 597†	256 273*	893 222	321·4
1959	338 147	13 077	—	393 433†	272 683*	1 017 340	366·0
1960	378 539	19 186	—	467 006†	292 345*	1 157 076	416·4
1961	396 755	22 398	—	551 607†	316 210*	1 286 970	463·0
1962	378 675	31 628	—	595 892†	343 059*	1 349 254	485·4
1963	459 679	54 040	12 302	675 190†	373 066*	1 574 277	566·4
1964	535 570	85 037	13 678	764 094†	369 083*	1 767 462	635·9
1965	549 594	141 718	11 228	828 235†	365 530*	1 896 305	678·3
1966	587 947	178 193	6997	857 614†	323 955*	1 954 706	703·2

Sources: College copies of 'Returns for Major Establishments' for 1951–2 to 1956–7. Thereafter the Ministry of Education no longer required statistcs of student hours and County returns were used for 1958–9 onwards.

* Figures exclude evening classes attended by part-time day students.
† Figures include evening classes attended by part-time day students.

Appendix II

Comparative Growth Rates: Jones College and England and Wales

In Student enrolments

	Number of enrolments			Growth Rates	
	1951–2	1956–7	1965–6*	1951–2 – 1956–7 (1951–2 = 100)	1956–7 – 1965–6 (1956–7 = 100)
All students					
England and Wales†	895 526	1 147 552	1 563 448	128·1	136·2
Jones College	2793	5031	9817†	180·1	195·1
Full-time					
England and Wales	40 821	63 809	141 591	156·3	221·9
Jones College	8	147	560	1837·5	380·9
Part-time day					
England and Wales	74 181	433 809	642 901	584·8	148·2
Jones College	812	1678	3264	206·7	194·5
Evenings only					
England and Wales	258 162	881 116	744 882	341·3	84·5
Jones College	1973	3206	5599	162·5	174·6

	Number of Enrolments		Growth rates
	1963–4	1965–6§	1963–4 – 1965–6
Sandwich			
England and Wales	18 622	25 613	137·5
Jones College	78	207	265·4
Short full-time			
England and Wales	5600	8861	158·2
Jones College	30	187	623·3

Sources: *For England and Wales:*

Education in 1952, Cmd. 8835, Table 35a, page 111. Education in 1957, Cmnd. 454, Table 48a, page 146.

Statistics of Education, Part 2, 1963, Table 5, page 37.

Statistics of Education, Part 2, 1964, Table 5, page 37.

Statistics of Education, Part 2, 1965, Table 15, page 39.

For Jones College:

Return for Major Establishments for Further Education, Form 13E, 1951–2 and 1956–7.

Department of Education and Science, Forms 107 and 108 FE, 1965–6.

* Until 1961–2 the statistics of student enrolments collected by the Ministry covered all enrolments and were submitted by colleges at the end of the academic year. Subsequently returns were based on students enrolled at the beginning of the academic year thus 'The figures of all students on the new basis (except in the case of sandwich students) are some 10 to 20 per cent over than those previously published.' (See Statistics of Education 1961, Part 2, page 21.) However, this does not disturb the comparability of Jones College and England and Wales.

† For 1951–2 and 1956–7 these are students included in the Ministry category 'Major Establishments' of further education. This category includes all grant aided further educational establishments except art establishments, evening institutes and residential adult education colleges. It excludes also full-time students in National Colleges. In comparing these years with 1965–6 the position was made difficult because of the transfer of new types of establishments to the further education statistics and the removal of colleges of advanced technology from them into the university sector statistics. With regard to the latter point, however, figures for CATs for 1964–5 were available and it is these that have been incorporated into the 1965–6 totals. Turning to the addition of new institutions, it was decided to exclude these where possible. Thus in terms of the Statistics for Education, Part 2, 1965, Table 15, the following have been included (in addition to the aforementioned CATs): National Colleges (excluding full-time students), Regional Colleges, Farm Institutes, Other Major Establishments and Direct Grant Establishments.

‡ This total is smaller than that in Table 1 because of the different basis used for the collection of statistics by the Department of Education compared with the County. The latter takes total enrolments at the *end* of the session and counts one student attending two courses twice. The Department, as mentioned above, takes its count at the beginning of the session and counts each student once only regardless of how many courses attended.

§ Figures for these courses are included in the total figures for 1965–6.

Appendix III

Extracts from an Interview with a Senior College Administrator

Q. Would you explain to me how policy is decided for the college,
that is, the nature of the relationship between the Principal,
the Governors and the local authority?

A. The Heads of Departments talk to the Principal and Vice-Principal.
They ought then to pass on matters to the Board of Governors but in
fact usually by-pass them and go straight to the Further Education
Officer. This is because the Education Officer is on the Board of
Governors himself . . . and in this way they cover two stages. The
matter will then be taken by him to the County Education Committee
or, if it is a financial matter, it will go to the Finance Committee.

Q. What has been the policy with regard to courses?

A. Until recently there has been no policy about what we should do and
what . . . College, for instance, should do. A couple of years ago a
Course Co-ordinating Committee was set up to consider what should
be held and where. This is an advisory body only though.

Q. For inter-county course policy?

A. There is nothing official, merely *ad hoc* meetings, for instance with
. . . County Council.

Q. What power has the Governing Body?

A. This is really an advisory body, representing the college to the
Education Committee. All the changes have come from the college
. . . It does wield some influence over small things, but the major
things come from the college. The Governing Body are just a bunch
of amateurs, or perhaps one should say enthusiasts . . . .

Q. What are the chief problems that arise out of the present administrative
structure?

A. Industry and Commerce haven't really an influential voice in what's
happening in the college. For example, the Advisory Committees
should be influential but the tendency is for industry to be represented
by middle or lower management. The representatives on the
Governing Body are nominated by the Chamber of Commerce and by
the Trades Council. (The Chairmen of the Advisory Committees are
usually members of the Governing Body so as to act as links.) These
bodies, the Chamber of Commerce and the Trades Council, don't
appoint at a high enough level. Not only that, but they are not
fully representative of industry, because not all the industries in the
locality are fully paid up members and because the Chamber of
Commerce represent local industry only. Nobody speaks for Shipping
Federation courses, yet we hold them here. We have Work Study
courses that are geared to a national basis but nobody speaks for
them.

Q. What is the answer to this?

A. We get round this by negotiating directly with large firms . . .

Q. Does this annoy the Governors?

A. They don't realise what goes on. They don't understand. The real policy making is done before they ever meet. That's why they only deal with the minor points at meetings. They don't understand the major issues and therefore they alight on the small things that catch their eye in the circulated reports, things they may be able to say something about, such as judo mats or muffle furnaces. The real issues escape discussion.

Q. Where did the CNAA application stem from?

A. From individual departments. The Heads of Departments would bring this up with the Principal who would then discuss the matter with the Advisory Committees. From there it would go to the Governors and then an application would be made to the Regional Advisory Committee and on to the CNAA. Then for a financial grant to the Department of Education and Science.

A. (A digression) I think this college has grown up in the way it has because certain personalities have made it grow this way. At one time there were big arguments about whether we should do management courses here. At the time they were only done at . . . (the neighbouring area college). They objected strongly to us doing them.

Q. Why is this? The former Principal had been here for a long time, I should have thought that there would have been a continuity of policy.

A. It is the *senior staff* who have shaped the college. This happens unless you have a Principal with a really dynamic personality.

Q. The recent statements put something of a stop to colleges determining their own ways . . . do you think this is a good thing?

A. Yes. Far too much money has been wasted on promoting courses that should not have been promoted. There has been far too much competition for students. It would have been far better if decisions had been made years ago at the outset. Things would, I think, have been much better had there been planning . . . If it had not been for a few personalities in the college, we should not be where we are.

Q. Is there any attempt on the Principal's or your part to keep a balance between the departments?

A. Well, we try to but some people have more forceable personalities than others. Some senior staff are quite prepared to sit back and go on doing the same thing that they have been doing for years.

Appendix IV

The Main Teaching Staff Sample

On the first of September, 1965, the effective size of the full-time teaching staff[1] of Jones College (effective here means ignoring unfilled vacancies) was 215. During the session, 28 of these resigned thereby leaving a population of 187.

Given that our aim was to interview in depth, we felt that it was not possible to see all 187 members of staff. It seemed to us that the task would be lightened if the Department of Art and Catering was omitted from the survey altogether. It contained certain somewhat unique characteristics as a college department; for example, the training of its students in the college refectories, which, though interesting in themselves, would have been time-consuming to pursue and may not have added a commensurate amount to our understanding of the college as a whole. This omission reduced numbers to 156. We decided to take one-third of these and ultimately interviewed 57 people. Two people from the sample originally selected expressed doubts about participation and although they were not completely opposed to doing so the matter was not pressed. In making our choice of a sampling criterion we were of course making a far more basic decision about the structure of the research project itself. Our problem was that we were not attempting to discover the relationship between a specific variable, say length of service, and attitudes and behaviour but conducting an exploratory study of attitudes and behaviour. If a straightforward random sample had been made, perhaps on the basis of the initial letters of surnames, it was possible that certain seemingly important elements would have been lost because of their statistical insignificance. The concern here was about small departments and senior members of staff particularly.

In the end the method adopted was that of selecting, by the initial letter of surnames, one person in three within each grade and by departments. In cases where there was only one person in a grade, and this frequently happened at principal and senior lecturer levels, the person was automatically included in the sample since his importance in the structure of the college clearly outweighed his numerical insignificance. If there were only two people in a grade, or two remained over, one was included. The Management and Professional Studies Department posed a particular problem in that it covered an extremely wide spectrum of disciplines – and indeed, as we have noted elsewhere, it was later to be divided into separate departments. The higher proportion of senior staff interviewed in that department is the result of an attempt to cover all its sections: in fact eleven senior people were selected but two of these (the two referred to earlier) did not participate.

[1] The Principal, Vice-Principal and Heads of Departments are not included here.

The Sample

Department	Teaching Staff, 1965–66			Sample		
	Senior*	Lecturer†	Total	Senior*	Lecturer†	Total
Engineering	10	28	38	4	10	14
Building	0	10	10	0	4	4
Science	7	16	23	3	5	8
Management	22	32	54	9	11	20
General Studies	2	29	31	1	10	11
Total	41	115	156	17	40	57

* This category includes both principal and senior lecturers.
† This category includes both lecturers and assistant lecturers.

Appendix V

The Interviewing Schedule†

A   Background Information

1. Name ....

2. Department ....

3. Date appointed...

4. Grade appointed at ....
   Grade at Sept. 1965 ....
   Grade at Sept. 1966 ....

5. (a)   Courses teaching on during the 1966–7 session
      ....

   (b)   Subjects taught during the session
      ....

6. Qualifications
   ....

7. Membership of professional bodies:
      name of body ....
      grade of membership ....
      elected by examination or exemption ....

8. Teacher training (details as to length, full-time, part-time)
   ....

9. Experience prior to Jones College appointment, in chronological order.
   ....

10. Date of birth...

B   Attitudes to Teaching

11. What made you decide to
      *(a)   enter further education from university/training college?
      *(b)   transfer from a school to further education?
      *(c)   transfer from industry/commerce to teaching in further
            education?

126

12. *(a)   Why did you decide to do without teacher training?
    *(b)   You decided to take a teacher training course, would you make the same decision again in the light of subsequent experiences?

13. *(a)   Would you consider teaching in a secondary school?
    *(b)   Would you consider returning to teach in a secondary school?

14.   Would you like to teach in a university?

15.   In financial terms, are you   better
                                         as well
                                         or worse off
      in further education than you would be in
                                    *(a)   a school?
                                    *(b)   in industry, etc.?

16.   Do you envisage remaining in the technical college field?

17.   (a)   Did you apply for any jobs during the last session?
     *(b)   Were they in further education, industry or commerce?

C   *Attitudes to the Job in General*
18.   (a)   How closely does the daily work you find yourself actually doing compare with what you feel your job should be:
                                    very closely?
                                    moderately closely?
                                    or is there no comparison?
      (b)   In what ways does it fail to match up to your ideal?

19.   What do you enjoy about working at Jones?

20.   What are you irritated by at Jones?

21.   When you first entered further education were you surprised by anything you found? In other words, did everything fit your preconceived notions or were certain things unexpected?

22.   What proportion of your time in college, estimating roughly, would you say you spend on administration of one kind and another, as against teaching and preparation?

127

23. Given a choice between the following two jobs at the same grade, which would you prefer:

> Job *X* with the emphasis on teaching and class contact
>
> or
>
> Job *Y* with the emphasis on the organisation and administration of courses?

24. Is there anything you would like to add to complete the following sentences?
    (a) I could teach better if . . .
    (b) I could carry out the various administrative parts of the job more easily and effectively if . . .

25. As you see it, what is the avenue of promotion in the college? In other words, what is the way to get on?

D. *Curricula, Students and Further Education*

26. The new Industrial Training Act anticipates a large-scale increase in the number of students attending technical colleges. Do you believe that such expansion will be of great benefit to the economy or are you dubious about the contribution to industrial and commercial activity this will make?

27. Do you agree with the idea that all school-leavers should receive further education of some kind?

28. It has been said that many students released by their firms waste their time when they are in the college, and look upon attendance as a soft option to a day at work. In your experience, what proportion of the released students do waste their time?

29. Do you find that the syllabuses that you have to teach by are usually in line with the professed objects of the course?

30. On the subject of courses, of those offered by the college last year,
    (a) were there any that you would not have put on personally?
    (b) on the other hand, were there any that you feel should have been tried?

31. There is a great deal of controversy over whether technical colleges should confine themselves to teaching specific skills for use in industrial and commercial life, or whether they should play a part in providing education of the more general kind, designed to cultivate 'the whole man'. Very often this controversy is reduced to a question of whether or not liberal studies should be included in a technical college's curricula. Do you agree with either of the following statements:

> Students' minds should be broadened with the aid of liberal studies periods in their curricula.
> A technical college is a place for teaching industrial and commercila skills and time should not be used up in teaching liberal studies.

E *Reference Groups, Staff and Departmental Association*

32. (a) Are you a member of the ATTI?
   *(b) Have you been, or are you, an official of some kind?

33. Did you attend
   (a) the Staff Association's Christmas celebration?
   (b) its summer dance?

34. (a) How often do you invite members of staff home, or do you go to their homes:
   > so far, never?
   > hardly ever?
   > occasionally?
   > frequently?
   *(b) Do these visitors consist of:
   > one or two close friends?
   > a circle of up to about 7 or 8?
   > or a larger circle?
   *(c) Are these visitors members of your own department exclusively, or do some of them work in other departments?

35. How much contact with members of other departments do you have in the process of arranging courses, dealing with firms and students or other college business:
   > a great deal?
   > some?
   > hardly any?
   > none?

36. How often do you invite students home:
    so far, never?
    hardly ever?
    occasionally?
    frequently?

37. (a) Are you working for any further qualifications?
    *(b) Why?

38. (a) Have you published anything?
    *(b) Do you intend to at some time?

39. Do you feel that publication has any bearing on your career prospects in further education?

40. Do you have any contact with the business world
    (a) on behalf of the college?
    (b) on your own account?

41. From which direction do you expect your chances of career advancement to come, from inside Jones or from outside?

F Structure and Administration of the College

42. As you know, during the year the college applied for recognition by the CNAA. Do you think that the college should aim at providing full-time, or sandwich, degree courses?

43. As you know also, under the recently published plan for re-organising the technical college structure, the college could conceivably lose its HND and similar level full-time and sandwich courses. How do you feel about that?

44. (a) Do you agree with the idea of transferring the college's lower level work to a junior college?
    *(b) Up to and including which level of courses would you like to see transferred?
    *(c) Would you mind being transferred to the college along with any course with which you were associated?

45. (a) Have you been responsible for organising any short courses since you came to Jones?

*(b) How did the decision to put on these short courses come about: were you approached about organising them or did you put forward the initial suggestion?

*(c) Were you asked to put on *a* short course, leaving you to choose the topic, or were you *given* a specific topic?

*(d) When you put forward the initial suggestion, was this a suggestion that there should be more short courses generally, or did you ask if you could put on a short course on a specific topic?

46. (a) The number of short courses offered by the college has increased rapidly during the past few years; are you in favour of this expansion?

    *(b) Do you believe that the college suffers any ill-effects from running them?

47. It has been suggested that the individual's incentive for running short courses is the possibility that promotion may lie at the end of it. Would you
    agree
    partially agree
    or disagree
    with this suggestion?

48. We all have our own ideas about how things should be run. If you were made Head of a Department are there any policies or methods of running the department that you would be particularly keen to introduce or use?

49. (a) Do you feel that the college is fulfilling its rightful function?
    (b) What is your interpretation of its function?

† As mentioned in the Introduction, these questions were used as guidelines and thus they do not represent the complete context of interaction between interviewer and respondent. For instance, follow-ups to questions were normally made although they have not always been indicated in the schedule.
    * These questions were asked only in the appropriate cases.